Hotel Management

HOTEL MANAGEMENT

Harish Bhatt

Crescent
CRESCENT
PUBLISHING CORPORATION

[*The responsibility for the facts stated, conclusions reached and plagiarism, if any, in this book is entirely that of the Author. And the Publisher bears no responsibility for them, whatsoever.*]

Hotel Management

First Published : 2006

ISBN 81-8342-001-X

Published by :

CRESCENT PUBLISHING CORPORATION
4831/24, Prahlad Street,
Ansari Road, Darya Ganj,
New Delhi - 110002
Ph. : 23272541, 23257835
Fax : 91- 011- 23257835
e-mail : campusbooks@hotmail.com

Typesetting by :

Arjun Computers
Delhi - 110051

Printed at :
S.P. Printech
Delhi

Preface

Hotel management is the art of managing, directing, facilitating or ascertaining the successful accomplishment of tasks or the attainment of stated objectives of a hotel. The operation of hotels, motels, and other lodging facilities presents unique problems for managers. The present volume is an introduction to hotel management which prepares students to succeed in entry-level management positions and provides the solid foundation needed to rise through the ranks and enjoy a long and successful career.

The book addresses the entire operation of a lodging facility, with an emphasis on the interrelationship between its departments. It covers everything from clear explanations of front office and housekeeping organization and staffing to detailed descriptions of procedures, such as reservations, registration, guest services, accounting, guest room cleaning, public area cleaning, inventory control, employee safety, and much more. It will serve as an ideal reference book for courses in hotel operations management, lodging operations management, rooms division, rooms management, front office operations management, guest services management, and lodging systems.

Harish Bhatt

Contents

1

Hotel and Tourism Management

Hotel management is art of managing, directing, facilitating or ascertaining the successful accomplishment of tasks or the attainment of stated objectives. In its simplest form management can best be described as that discipline designed and used to get tasks accomplished. This simple definition denigrates the fact that much of today's modern management theory is steeped in and has been developed from theories which were initially university-based. In Hotels, your security is generally based on how the fire is handled. However, many people do not know, or follow, correct procedures in coping with a fire. This is another step you, as a traveller, can take to protect yourself and your family. By choosing a secure hotel, you're choosing a well made, fire-resistant property.

However, many hotels abroad are not as fire-resistant as those here: it may be difficult to contact a fire department; there may not be reliable smoke detectors or sprinkler systems; there may be too few exits and escape routes may not be posted; escape routes may not be posted in hallways; and, fire-fighting equipment and water supplies may be limited. Experts tell us that if a fire starts, try to call the fire department or the police for help—do not rely on a security guard.

The hotel and tourism industry has been suffering particularly from the combined effects of a general economic downturn that began to show itself early in 2001 and the shock wave from the events on September 11 th of the same year. The general economic downturn had already started to reduce the industry's previously strong 4½ per cent annual growth rate to well below 4 per cent. The impact of the September 11 th events on tourism was dramatic. The whole industry lost an additional 10 per cent or more of its business worldwide, with certain countries experiencing falls of up to 30 per cent. The extreme market lows remained for at least three months, plunging the industry's growth rate for the whole year 2001 into negative territory of somewhere between -1 per cent and -5 per cent.

Although signs of a recovery have been observed since January 2002, it is proving slow to take hold. More recent events have raised new security concerns worldwide. They include the terrorist attacks in Bali, 12 October, and in Mombasa, 14 November 2002. The Moscow hostage drama, late October, also contributes to an increased feeling of insecurity in the international sphere as does the perspective of a possibly aggravating conflict in the Middle East. Forecasters had predicted that tourism would return to its pre-September 11th levels in 2003. Recent reports, however, of the renewed decline in the third quarter of 2002 of certain performance indicators, suggest that a longer recovery period is to be expected. A flat performance, i. e. continued stagnation, now seems more likely. Longer-term predictions now suggest that the industry's pre-2001 growth rates will not be regained before the year 2004 and that it will take the market until 2005 to get back to its - outstanding - year 2000 volume.

Employment figures in the sector have reacted more slowly to the crisis, but the negative effects will be longer lasting. Employers at first hesitated to reduce staff levels, although reducing costs on personnel through shorter hours and lower fringe benefits. The common tendency, particularly in the service sectors, is for staff lay-offs to be partially compensated by increased productivity. Consequently, the longer the crisis lasts, or the slower the industry recovers, the more jobs are lost irretrievably.

According to estimates by the World Travel and Tourism Council (WTTC), the events of September 11 th and subsequent developments will have caused more than six and a half million jobs to be lost in the travel and tourism industry over the years 2001 and 2002 - some 6.9% of the total employed, as compared to a normal growth that could have been expected in normal times without the impact of a crisis. This estimate does not include those related sectors providing inputs to travel and tourism, where employment may have suffered in similar proportions.

Although international tourism is generally highlighted for statistical convenience, the crisis has had an important impact on domestic tourism levels as well, particularly in the United States, where much of the internal tourism involves the use of air transport. Both international and domestic tourism tend to reflect the general level consumer confidence. Travel and tourism are the types of product on which consumers can easily make substantial savings if they need to, e.g. by purchasing lower quality services, by taking shorter leave or by spending their vacations closer to home. Adjustments like this have undoubtedly been made by consumers in order to adapt to the present increased economic and psychological pressures on travelling.

Nevertheless, there have been some initial signs of recovery in leisure tourism as can be observed in tour operators' business in early 2002. These signs serve, in a way, to illustrate both the extent to which leisure tourism suffered immediately following September 11 th and the fact that the crisis phase immediately thereafter in this particular sector seemed actually to be quite short. One contributing factor might have been that the promotional campaigns undertaken by the tourism industry to mitigate the negative effects of the crisis, accompanied by measures taken to support small enterprises. They have also had a much greater effect on leisure tourism than on business travel. However, general economic constraints continue to force consumers to apply various types of savings measures such as avoiding air transport, choosing cheaper destinations, staying for shorter periods of time, and booking late. Another point worth noting is that developing countries are not benefiting proportionately from any recovery in leisure tourism because of their heavy dependence on foreign tourists, and particularly on long-haul tourists.

Business travel (which falls under the generally accepted definition of tourism if one night is spent outside the usual living sphere) is recovering more slowly, if at all. Corporate travel professionals are not expecting to see a recovery in business travel for at least another year. Although in terms of numbers, business travellers may account for no more than one-fifth of the total travelling population, they contribute nearly one-half of the industry's total revenue because of their high frequency of travel. It has been observed that, in light of the economic downturn, travel managers of corporations and businesses are moving to renegotiate contracts in order to reduce business travel costs.

Most affected countries have taken measures on a central, regional or local level, aimed at mitigating the effects of the tourism crisis. To varying degrees, losses in long-haul international tourism have been successfully compensated by gains in international tourism from within a region. This is the case, for example, with certain European countries and with Canada, and some therefore ended the year 2001 registering positive growth in their levels of international tourism. Domestic tourism in many developed countries benefited from reduced outbound tourism because many clients who were previously long-haul tourists now favour surface travel, and cheaper, shorter trips.

Major and, at times, remarkable measures were taken to stimulate consumer demand and support the industry by sectoral bodies, including national tourist boards and ad hoc committees composed of tourism authorities and industry representatives in public-private partnerships. Governments have been participating financially in advertising campaigns, quality improvement programmes, tax relief schemes, or the granting of subsidies to small and medium-sized enterprises (SME's).

Despite the fact that the developments in tourism after 11 September 2002 are those of a crisis with a beginning and hopefully with an end, they seem to have introduced or at least accelerated lasting changes in consumer demand for tourism products. Specialists agree that patterns such as "sea, sand and sun" may get out of fashion as may the desire of many tourists to travel as far as possible and to places as exotic as possible. New trends show an inclination to stay closer to home and make sure that holidays are an "experience," be it in the area of cultural enrichment, in the area of sport or other. Providers are challenged to meet those specific types of demand by developing higher value products and at the same time compensate a tendency of consumers to spend less money. Developing countries are particularly challenged in order to compensate for long distance travel, language differences, and less complete infrastructure to receive tourists other than in beach resorts.

For most countries, knowledge of the volume of border crossing tourism is largely limited to the numbers of arrivals and the expenditure by international tourists in the host country published with varying delay by governments and presented annually by the World Tourism Organization (WTO). Some more frequent statistical surveys are carried out based on samples covering also domestic tourism and especially hotel performance indicators, but these do not produce figures representative of the total size of the industry. Only a dozen countries have so far started to develop statistical instruments to measure the whole tourist industry (Tourism Satellite Accounts), and at present results are published only after long delays. Estimates that are available are based on different methodologies and hardly comparable. When it comes to employment figures, however, there are hardly any other sources available.

Another complication is that definitions of the 'tourism' market or industry vary according to the particular perspectives of the different organizations. For example, is 'travel' included or not? (It is by the WTTC).

Impact of September 11

In 2001 until September 11 th, travel and tourism had been growing at the annual rate of 3.8 per cent and was expected to maintain that level of growth for the full year. In the event, according to WTTC estimates, travel and tourism demand worldwide in 2001 ended 1.3 per cent down on the previous year. The real decline for the whole of 2001 as compared to the expected growth was therefore 5.1 per cent, of which it has been estimated that as much as 4.4 percentage points can be attributed to September 11 th alone (85%).

In 2002, the year-on-year decline of travel and tourism was expected to continue, with WTTC forecasting last spring a slight decrease by 0.4 per cent for the whole of 2002. The forecast was adjusted in fall when WTTC estimated a flat performance as compared to 2001. On the assumption that last year's pre-September 11 th growth of 3.8 per cent would normally have continued throughout 2002, this would mean another real annual decline for tourism of close to 4 percent, of which around 3 percentage points can be attributed to the events of September 11 th alone (70%).

Receipts from cross-border tourism in 2001

The positive growth trend that prevailed throughout the 1990's was brought to an end in 2001 by a drop in the industry's income from international travellers of some 5.2 per cent at constant US Dollar prices. It should be noted that the receipts from international tourism dropped deeper than the number of international arrivals, shown in the next section, due to new general consumer preferences for shorter stays and cheaper services.

Border-crossing tourist arrivals in 2001

The number of international tourist arrivals worldwide fell by 0.6 per cent in the full year 2001, compared to the year 2000, but there were important differences between regions and countries both for the full year and for the four-month period after September 11. The worst losses were felt in the Middle East and the Americas, particularly North America, where international tourist arrivals were down by 6.8 per cent in the whole year 2001, but by as much as 22.6 per cent in the last four months compared to equivalent periods of the previous year.

Some more detailed figures published earlier by the World Tourism Organization provide the basis for an analysis of the impact of September 11 on specific countries. Countries most affected by the September 11 th events were the United States, with international tourist arrivals having fallen to their lowest point between September and November, on average over 30 per cent below the level of the same period the previous year. Countries in the immediate neighbourhood of the US also received significantly less tourists than at the same time the previous year, e.g. Canada: (-19%), Cuba (-26%), Dominican Republic (-25%), Mexico (-24%) and Jamaica (-20%).

In general, all countries that would normally have expected a high proportion of their incoming long-haul tourism to originate from the United States experienced steep declines in international tourism in the first three months following September 11. In Europe, those worthy of note include the United Kingdom (-12 %), Germany (-17%), Switzerland (-16%), Italy (-11%) and Austria (-9%) - and elsewhere, the Philippines (-25%) and Australia (-21%). Some other countries amongst those whose tourist industries are important elements in their national economies suffered badly such as Egypt (-55%), Tunisia (-25%) and Morocco (-22%). These preliminary figures served to confirm earlier predictions that the three types of tourist destinations likely to be most affected by the events of 2001 were:

— countries highly dependent on US outbound travel;
— destinations a long distance from their main generating markets; and
— countries of the Muslim world

In addition to security aspects, the general economic downturn in 2001 also contributed to the poorer performance of international tourism in 2001 compared to the previous year. Here, the main causes are to be found in those major sending countries such as the US, Germany, and Japan. South American markets suffered from economic instability in Argentina. An additional factor for the US as a receiving country, which lost as much as 2.5 per cent on international arrivals in the first nine months of the year, was its strong currency.

Among the countries performing worse as a destination for the full year 2001, compared to the year 2000, were the US (-12.6%), Argentina (-9%), Brazil (-8%), the UK (-6.6%), Mexico (-5%), Germany (-5.5%), Italy (-5%), the Dominican Republic (-5%), Jamaica and the Bahamas (both -4%). Other countries experienced a significant drop in their 2001 total tourist numbers year-on-year because, rightly or wrongly, they were associated with security risks, and this was for various reasons not necessarily connected to the September 11 th events. These countries included Egypt (-16%), Nepal (-22%), and Sri Lanka (-16%).

By contrast, there were some countries, notably in Europe bordering at the East Mediterranean Sea and in Southern Europe that in 2001 continued to receive higher numbers of foreign tourists than in the previous year, probably because they provide a convenient alternative to long-haul destinations for many European tourists. Thus Turkey (+12%), Croatia (+12%), Slovenia (+11%), Spain (+3%), Greece (+2%) and Cyprus (+1%) all benefited in 2001. It was also observed that several emerging tourist destinations in Europe showed strong growth in the full year 2001, notably Bulgaria (+14%), Slovakia (+13%) and Estonia (+9%). France (+1.2%) also recorded some growth in 2001 versus their previous year totals, benefiting from their familiarity and proximity with European holidaymakers and even compensating a temporary 20 per cent drop immediately following September 11 th which was probably due the sudden lack of Americans visiting Europe.

Australia and New Zealand reported a short period of decline in inbound tourism immediately after September 11 th , but most of these losses were partly offset by something of a boom in numbers of foreign tourists later in the year. Some countries, such as the UK, Germany, China and Canada continued to send record numbers of tourists to this part of the world throughout 2001. They did not prevent, however, a year-on-year decline of 2.7 per cent in numbers of international arrivals, mainly accounted for by 4 th quarter decreases from Japan (-28.9%) and the US (-17.5%).

Notably, the region with the best performance as tourist destination in 2001 was South East Asia and the Pacific, which in spite of a decline after 11 September still ended the year with a growth of 5.5 per cent, mainly due to intra-regional tourism. Performing regions were also Africa and Central America, albeit on a small basis in absolute terms.

The United States

The United States is the country whose hotel, travel and tourism industry was most seriously affected. According to the US Office of Travel and Tourism Industries, the total number of international arrivals fell by almost 11 per cent over the whole year 2001. This was largely because of a dramatic 30 per cent drop in September, moving to a 34.0 per cent loss in October, with an average 31.8 per cent loss of business over the last four months of the year compared to the same period of the previous year. October was the worst month. The numbers of international arrivals slowly started to recover in November (Table 1).

Table 1 Non-resident arrivals to the U.S.
By world region or country of residence
2001

	Total	Canada	Total overseas
Change from same period the year before (per cent)			
October	-34.0	-24.3	-39.3
November	-29.2	-21.0	-34.1
4 th Quarter	-31.8	-22.8	-36.9
Year 2001*	-10.7	-7.8	-13.67
Count (million)			
Year 2001*	45,5	13,5	22,4

Certain countries supplying travellers to the US performed worse than others because they were more seriously affected by economic crises. These included Brazil (-49%); Germany (-46%) and Japan (-45%). But all of the top 10 markets experienced steep falls of around 20 per cent or more, as is shown in Table 2 below. By the end of the year, however, it was the German market that had performed worse than any other, which is probably due to generally nervous consumer behaviour in the light of the country's poor economic performance.

Table 2. Top 10 markets for tourism to the US Arrivals Change in 2001 and projection for 2002

2001/2000 (Sept.)	Year 2001/2000	Year 2002/2001	Count 2001

	(Per cent)	(Per cent)	(Per cent)	(million)
Canada	-19	-7.8	0.9	13.5
Mexico	-30	-7.4	2.6	9.6
United Kingdom	-27	-10.7	1.5	4.2
Japan	-45	-18.5	-3.6	4.1
Germany	-46	-24.6	-1.6	1.3
France	-34	-14.0	-1.6	0.9
South Korea	-20	-5.3	5.1	0.6
Brazil	-49	-22.7	-1.2	0.6
Venezuela	-21	-1.1	-8.6	0.6
Italy	-40	-19.8	3.7	0.5
Total international		-10.7	-0.1	45.5

Demand for accommodation in the US is estimated to have suffered a far more modest decline than international arrivals, another indication that domestic tourism was less affected and it was long-haul travel that suffered most. Accommodation demand had already declined by 6.0 per cent in the third quarter of 2001, as compared to the same period in 2000. However, the decline in the fourth quarter was markedly greater (6.5%), but still only a fifth of the decline in international arrivals.

Early forecasts by the Travel Industry Association of America already suggested that after the 7.6 per cent drop in 2001, the recovery in consumer expenditure levels on travel in the US would be slow in 2002, with an annual growth rate of only 2.2 per cent. Leisure trips in March, April and May 2002, for example, were 4 per cent below the level in the same period a year ago.

Overall, first quarter 2002 international arrivals to the US were down 12 per cent (8.3 million compared to 9.5 million in 2001). Four of the top markets - the United

Kingdom, Germany, the Netherlands and Switzerland - posted declines for the first quarter of 2002, but the declines are less than those recorded in the pre-September 11 th months in 2001. Mexico and Spain are the main markets posting positive growth in numbers of arrivals through the first quarter 2002, at +22 per cent and +6 per cent respectively versus the same period last year.

Recovery in the US is not being enjoyed equally by all sub-sectors of the industry. Leisure tourism services are recovering faster, for example, than the sub-sector catering for business travellers. In both the US and in Canada, where large advertising campaigns featured domestic attractions, resort destinations are being filled by leisure tourists driving their cars instead of flying. However, on another dimension, according to a sample of hotels monitored in the USA (40-42), the full-service hotels suffered a decline in their Revenue per Available Room (RevPAR) of 13.5 per cent in the first six months of 2002, although operating expenses were reduced by 9.1 percent as compared to the same period in 2001. Profits (defined as income before deductions for capital reserves, rent, interest, income taxes, depreciation, and amortization) declined as much as 21 per cent.

The Marriott hotel chain had publicized similar results at an earlier stage. The continued decline in the more profitable business travel had forced its RevPAR down by an average of 12.7 per cent. Marriott said its earnings for the first quarter 2002 were down 32 per cent versus a year earlier, on income that had dropped by 4 per cent. The US accommodation industry is estimated to save US$3.4 billion in 2002 through cost-cutting measures that were put in place in 2001. Without these actions, profits would have decreased by 18.5 per cent to US$13.7 billion in 2002. However, more recent developments seem to limit recovery expectations for

2002. The negative wealth effect of the recent sharp decline in stock values, the general erosion in consumer confidence in the US, increasing frustration with the inconvenience of air travel and heightened fears of a war against Iraq, will restrain lodging demand growth and encourage continued discounting through the end of 2002.

Marriott reports, for US properties across its lodging brands, a decline in RevPAR by an average of as high as 6.8 percent in the 2002 third-quarter. Price water house Coopers forecast RevPAR in the US to decline by 2.3 percent this year but to increase by 3.5 percent in 2003. The more robust outlook for lodging has, however, been delayed to 2004. In particular the business travel industry is forecast to continue its downward move this year with income falling 4.3 per cent. It is expected to stabilize in 2003 with a gain of still less than 1 per cent. Overall travel expenditures in the US are expected to virtually stagnate in 2002 and strengthen to an annual growth rate of 5.0 per cent by 2003 (Table 3 below), reaching US$555.6 billion, still below that of the year 2000.

Table 3 Travel Expenditures in the United States

	2000	2001	2002	2003
Total (US$ billion)	570.5	537.2	535.3	555.6
Annual Growth (per cent)	7.1	- 5.8	-0.4	5.0

Source: Travel Industry Association of America (TIA), October 2002

The Travel Industry Association of America observed that by August 2002 the annual rate of decline in US hotel and motel receipts was running at - 1.3 per cent. However, the trend was positive, because the decline was as high as - 5.9 per cent for the month of June 2002. The decline in the level of employment in hotels and motels, however, improved at a slower pace, with as high as - 4.7 per cent in August against - 5.2 per cent in June. Employment in eating and drinking places fell by -1.8 per cent in August, even worse than in than in June (-1.3) and contrasting with the positive, albeit equally declining, levels of growth in receipts of 3.7 per cent and 5.5 per cent respectively.

The drop in outbound tourism from the USA is still being felt in many countries, but most strongly in Europe. The number of American tourists in France in April 2002 was almost one-third less than in the same month a year earlier. In the United Kingdom, the number of American tourists in the early months of 2002 was 10 per cent less than in 2000 - the last "normal" year before a combination of foot-and-mouth disease and fears of terrorism sent American and most other visitor numbers into free fall. And the number of American visitors was down 11 per cent in the first half of this year in Rome, Florence, Venice and Naples, compared to the same period a year before.

Japanese travel agents indicating that by November 2001 they had suffered a drop of 21 per cent in their total business since September 11 th . They reported a record level of cancellations representing 52.1 per cent of all the overseas package tours with departure dates between September and November. The number of Japanese travelling abroad was down 9.1 per cent at the end of 2001 versus the previous year, according to a report released in January 2002.

Whereas in May 2002 the number of bookings of foreign trips through Japan's top 50 travel agencies was still 6 per cent less than the previous year, July and August, the peak season, have been especially slow, with 10 to 20 per cent fewer bookings than in the previous year. By contrast, the numbers of visitors to domestic destinations were up by 4.6

per cent to 2.07 million. In the period immediately following September 11 th , the largest travel agent (JTB) saw an increase of 19 per cent in their bookings for domestic tours departing during the October-December period.

Table 4. Travellers within, to, and from Japan

	2001 estimate		2002 prediction	
	Thousands	Growth (per cent)	Thousands	Growth (per cent)
Total	341,310	-0.6	340,130	-0.3
Domestic Travellers	325,110	-0.1	323,490	-0.5
Overseas Visitors to Japan	4,730	-0.6	5,140	8.7
Travellers to Overseas Destinations	16,200	-9.1	16,640	2.7

China experienced some impressive growth in both domestic and inbound tourism, with domestic tourism developing particularly strongly. Total annual revenue from tourism has grown on average by 12.7 per cent over recent years, much faster than the gross domestic product (GDP) which grew by an average rate of 7.4 per cent. More than 73.34 million overseas tourists visited China during the first 10 months of 2001, an increase of 5.7 per cent on the same period of 2000, or almost double the world's average growth rate for 2001 before September 11 th . The total amount spent by overseas tourists in that period grew by 9.3 per cent to US$14.8 billion. Over two-thirds of the revenue is still, however, from domestic tourism.

Spain's tourist industry, which directly employs more than a million people and accounts for 12 per cent of the economy, is suffering a protracted crisis, recording 10 per cent less visitors for the first six months of 2002 compared to the same period the previous year. The number of German visitors to Spain in July 2002 was 20 per cent lower, pushing down the hotel occupancy rate by 5.5 per cent. Reservations made by German tour operators tumbled by as much as 37 per cent. The crisis is attributed partly to growing unemployment in Germany, but also to price increases in Spain, with German tourists preferring cheaper destinations such as Turkey and Croatia.

In Switzerland, tourist numbers for the six-month winter season 2001-02 were a dramatic 6 per cent down on the previous year's winter season result. Yet this was still 1.4 per cent above the average for the previous five winter seasons. Increased domestic tourism seems to have stepped in to replace international visitors, whose numbers dropped by 10 per cent. The number of tourists visiting from the US was nearly 20 per cent less and from Japan 31 per cent less than in the same period the year before.

Overnight trips to Canada were up by 0.6 per cent for the first five months of 2002 compared to the same period in 2001, boosted by an increase in US travellers entering Canada by car (accounting for 9.9% of the total). On the other hand, the number of Canadian tourists to the US or overseas was still down by 7.2 per cent (at 1.5 million) in May 2002, which represented something of a recovery because it was down 11.3 per cent for the five months before, compared to the same period a year ago.

The government of Morocco predicts that tourism revenues will have dropped by US$700 million by the end of 2002, down by one-quarter on the total revenue of US$2.7 million reached in 2001. Morocco's tourist industry recorded a 43 per cent revenue drop in January 2002 compared to January 2001. The industry currently employs over half a million people, serving some 2.4 million foreign tourists annually.

Major markets supplying most of Australia's tourists showed dramatic falls in outbound tourism during the 12 months to July 2002, with the number of visitors from neighbouring New Zealand dropping by 25.5 per cent, from the UK by 17.7 per cent and the United States by 8.4 per cent, according to the Australian Bureau of Statistics. Overall, international visitor arrivals have fallen 8.4 per cent to 409,400 from January to July 2002, compared to the 446,900 tourists for the same period last year. These results were attributed September 11 th mainly, but Australian tourism leaders feel under pressure by the lasting downturn, leading them to reconsider their whole marketing strategy. A return to pre-September 11 th levels of international arrivals was still seen as being a long way off.

After the bomb attack of October 2002, the Australian tourism industry fears negative effects of tourists avoiding Asia. Singapore and Bangkok are stopovers on the most popular route from Europe to Australia. Any disruption to the flow of tourists to them would have a severe knock-on effect on Australia. Industry reports in late October 2002, however, suggested the tourist numbers from all markets would remain largely unaffected as a result of the 12 October Bali attacks.

Employment in the Tourism Sector

Employment numbers in the tourism sector do not react immediately to a decrease in business because the special characteristics of employment relationships in the sector allow for some labour cost reduction to take place before workers finally become unemployed. Flexible working arrangements such as part-time or on-call working are common for at least one quarter of the labour force and help to avoid their complete unemployment in a business crisis, albeit with reduced income. Employees accounting for almost another quarter of the total have full time but temporary employment contracts and are the first victims of formal unemployment when reducing their working time and income becomes insufficient to address the income crisis of the enterprise. Employers usually hesitate, however, to reduce their core of trained staff. Only if a crisis persists, businesses tend to restructure and workers are eventually laid off permanently. Jobs then remain lost, even in times of recovery.

WTTC estimates a 7.4 per cent drop in tourism demand over the years 2001 and 2002 combined, instead of the 3.8 per cent growth that had been anticipated previously for each of these two years. The sector is now seen as being in a state of stagnation, which is a dramatic change in fortune considering its previously very high growth rate. The WTTC estimated that over 6 million jobs would have been lost in the tourism industry worldwide in the years 2001 and 2002, which represent 8.6 per cent of employees, or one in every 12 jobs in the industry.

The process of attempting to derive employment estimates from demand estimates has to take into account that normal growth may not result in increased employment because normal growth is achieved largely through gains in labour productivity. WTTC estimated therefore that a growth of demand by 3.8 per cent would have entailed a growth of employment by only 2 per cent. Given this proportion, the dramatic effects on employment forecasted by WTTC can be better appreciated.

WTTC foresees a modest recovery of employment in the travel and tourism industry worldwide in 2003. However, with a growth of 1.7, the year 2003 will still end with a 6.4 million jobs lost as a result of the crisis compared to the expected normal annual growth rate of 2 per cent in that year.

The Travel Industry Association of America (TIA) estimates that 19 million Americans were employed directly or indirectly by the travel industry, with an annual payroll of $174 billion. The year 2001 ended with domestic travel volumes and expenditure down 3.5 per cent and 7 per cent respectively, and volumes and expenditure from international travel to the US down 12.6 per cent and 11.2 per cent respectively. Employment in the whole industry in the USA was down 5.8 per cent for the year, with an estimated 1.1 million jobs lost.

High volume tourist destinations such as Las Vegas, Orlando and Honolulu are expected to have suffered major losses in 2002 due to cutbacks in travel. Among 315 metro areas examined by the Milken Institute at the end of 2001, many jobs would be lost as a result of the events after 11 September 2001 in New York, Los Angeles and other big cities. A ranking of industries (at the 3-digit level of the International Standard Classification of Industries) most affected by job losses after September 11 th shows the hotel and catering sector represented by the top two categories listed (see Table 5). The Milken Institute forecasted heavy job losses for the years to come as well, although at a decreasing rate. Over two-thirds of the estimated 760,000 total direct jobs expected to be lost in US metropolitan areas were in core sectors related to travel and tourism.

Table 5. Net Job Losses in 315 Metropolitan Areas of the United States (Thousands)

	2001	2002	2003	2004
Eating & Drinking Places	-17.95	-150.56	-174.18	-105.22
Hotels & Motels	-49.17	-140.61	-99.40	-38.64
Miscellaneous Amusement & Recreational Services	-33.00	-100.36	-76.28	-42.30
Scheduled Air Transportation	-46.16	-85.89	-35.19	-28.63
Total of core tourism related sectors	-145.83	-477.42	-385.05	-214.79
Total Job Loss (all sectors)	-172.53	-758.92	-587.07	-340.97

Taking a longer-term view, it may be concluded that the September 11 th events merely served to exacerbate an already established downward trend by adding, for a limited time only, some extra ingredients such as the perception of heightened insecurity. The general economic downturn in 2001 had already started to affect all forms of consumption and travel and tourism was probably one of the sectors that suffered most because it is a market in which consumers can easily make savings. Indeed, future variations in the level of consumer expenditure on tourism will probably be driven mainly by variations in levels of present and expected household income.

The Travel Industry Association of America (TIA) undertook three Travel Confidence Surveys in the US, one from 21 to 22 September, another from 12 to 13 October 2001 and the third from 2 to 4 November 2001. In these polls, only 14 per cent of respondents cited safety as their top travel concern. On the other hand, 42 per cent cited economic concerns as reasons for not travelling. Nonetheless, the fear factor continued well into 2002 as a strong deterrent to travel in the US and the health of the industry continued to be affected by federal alerts, air-travel-related accidents and other concerns.

A German survey of 8,000 households showed that in March 2002 only one person in ten claimed to make travel decisions on the basis of security considerations, compared to November 2001 when the proportion had been almost one person in three.

It has been predicted that tourism would recover slowly and regain the levels of before September 11 th by the third or fourth quarter of 2002. This forecast would be in line with experiences from previous security crises affecting tourism, albeit local, whose effects lasted for about one seasonal cycle. The continuing economic slowdown in the western world, as well as more recent terrorist activities targeting tourists in Djerba, Bali and Mombasa, however, are having an added effect on the tourism crisis. The year 2002 has been one of rather little growth or even slight decline of tourism performance indicators, with the possible exceptions of the Asian Pacific region and South Africa which has recorded double digit growth of tourism out of Europe in 2002, or China which does continues to grow rapidly both as a destination and as a market.

Estimates by large tour operators are usually good indicators of the volume of business in leisure tourism, which represents roughly two-thirds of all travel and tourism activities. Preussag, a major German tour operator, was expecting the poor performance of the winter season 2001-2002 improve for the summer season. By June 2002, however, summer bookings in Germany were down 14.2

per cent on a year earlier, even worse than in winter, when total Preussag bookings were down by 10.9 per cent.

Surprisingly, the German Travel Agents and Tour Operators Federation expected much better results in financial terms than in numbers of bookings, which suggests a scenario of structural changes in the leisure travel business leading towards higher quality demand. According to German tour operators, because of higher price levels, total turnover for the 2000/01 season which ended in October grew by twice as much (+ 6.8%) as the number of bookings (+3.2%), reaching a total of Euro17.4 billion. For 2002, despite bookings being down, German tour operators expected a turnover close to that of 2001, mainly because certain customers are making higher value choices even if they go for shorter stays.

In general, tourism demand was in the last 12 months or so subject to important structural changes including a re-distribution of demand between countries and regions. Leisure destinations located close to important markets have prospered; domestic tourism has made a difference; long-distance international air transport has suffered more than international tourism in general due to increased short distance trips across borders; business tourism and conventions, luxury hotels, and cruises during the winter season were particularly affected, while social tourism, rural tourism, rail and road travel made gains. This is why the decline in business revenues was generally sharper than the decline in the number of travellers.

Among the destinations receiving European tourists, short-haul destinations have generally benefited at the expense of long-haul destinations, with demand for North America showing the greatest fall in 2002 so far (-13%). The main long-haul destination to buck the trend has been

China, but a number of other Asian destinations and South Africa have similarly recorded double-digit growth out of Europe this year.

International arrivals to countries in the European region will show little change in 2002 over last year which closed with a decrease of -0.6% in international tourist arrivals in Europe. Preliminary figures for the first six to eight months of 2002 indicate a small decrease in the region of -0.2% to -0.3%). As of November 2002, preliminary results show that Northern Europe has suffered the biggest decline in tourist arrivals in Europe. The other sub- regions have been more successful, especially the Mediterranean countries and 'new' destinations such as Turkey, Croatia and Bulgaria.

Austria, as a typical short haul destination for European markets saw foreign leisure arrivals grow by a massive 12% in the first half of 2002. This growth, however, is expected to have eased to a rate of only around 2% for the whole year.

For France, preliminary data on international arrivals (classified hotel accommodation only) suggest that the lucrative US market remained down by no less than a fifth in the first eight months of 2002 as compared to the same period in 2001, whilst growth in the Canadian market was replaced by decline. All international arrivals together performed at a low 0.5 per cent growth, as the performance of the major generating markets within Europe has been considerable with tourists from the UK (almost half of foreign clients of classified hotels) increasing by close to 7 per cent, and arrivals from Germany (another quarter) still increasing by 14 per cent. The nascent trend towards short-haul, short - break holidays seems to be re-configuring the intra-regional European market, with France being perhaps the main beneficiary.

Germany as a destination lost 3.3% in the number of foreign overnight stays for the first half of 2002, according to preliminary data, which, however, was still 0.2% higher than in the same period in 2000. Most of the loss is due a decrease in long haul tourists such as from the Americas (-14.6 %). Arrivals from within Europe suffered much less and still grew by 0.9 per cent. Those markets whose growth is worthy of mention in the first six months of 2002 are the Netherlands (2.9%), Switzerland (4.0%) and Norway (6.7%), Russia (9.3%) and China (13.1%). Still, Germany remains out of favour with some important markets, such as the UK (-6.7%), France (-3.4%), and Italy (-2.3%).

Foreign travellers to Italy remarkably did not decline substantially, but expenditures did. They dropped by as much as 11 per cent in the first six months of 2002 as compared to the same period in 2001. This phenomenon is likely to exist also elsewhere, but figures on 2002 are still scarce. A slight growth of foreign arrivals to Italy is anticipated for the remainder of 2002 which will close with a growth of 0.9 per cent.

Tourist arrivals at Spain's frontiers increased in the first two quarters of 2002 by comfortable 6.9 percent, but only by 0.2 per cent in the second quarter as compared to the same periods in 2001. The summer period may not have been any better. It was, however, in the United Kingdom, where after a weak winter and spring period, July 2002 arrivals exceeded those of the year before by as high as 15 per cent and even those of July 2000. Expenditure increased less, but still by 7 per cent. Estimates on the whole of 2002 see arrivals increase by comfortable 6 per cent, but expenditure by as high as 9 per cent indicating that off season tourists spend more money than the (younger) summer holiday travellers.

Canada had continued growing as a destination for foreign tourists during the crisis year 2001, albeit at a slower pace, since most of foreign travellers came from the USA and increasingly used surface transport, in part substituting Canada for a long haul destination elsewhere. In the first six months of 2002, however, the number of foreign tourists from the USA slightly shrunk (by 0.2 per cent), and the receiving of overseas tourism, which had been down in 2001 by 8.4 per cent (arrivals) and 4 per cent (expenditures) continued declining by 13 per cent (arrivals), reducing anticipated overall growth of foreign arrivals in 2002 to only 0.1per cent.

Japan receives one international traveller only for five Japanese outbound tourists. Out of the modest number of less than 5 million that do arrive, it is estimated that over a quarter are in Japan on business and that half of this market originates from Asia. Having suffered in 2001 only a slight 0.3 per cent decrease of the annual growth rate for all tourism, with a higher growth rate for leisure tourists of 0.9 per cent, Japan is estimated to benefit in 2002 from an impressive growth in foreign arrivals of 16 per cent, to a large extent due to an increase of the number of tourists from China. Outbound tourism from Japan, important for many destinations in the world, is currently forecast to record modest growth in 2002 of a maximum 1-2% after a 9% decline in 2001.

The Pacific Asian countries have been doing well as destinations in spite of the world crisis in 2001 and 2002. High GDP performances in mainland China, India and South Korea suggest the trend of Asian intra-regional tourism will continue. India as a source country appears to record strong double-digit growth in 2002, albeit on a small basis. Inbound tourism in India, however, after dropping in 2001 by a moderated 4.2 per cent (arrivals) and 5.5 percent (expenditures), continues suffering from the conflict with Pakistan and the closeness to Afghanistan.

Northeast and Southeast Asia are driving the region's growth - both as destinations and as markets. During 2001, almost 65% of international visitor arrivals in Northeast Asia came from within Northeast & Southeast Asia. For destinations within Southeast Asia the proportion was over 64%. China has continued to show strong growth in 2002. In the first eight months of 2002 foreign arrivals in mainland China increased by more than 16%. Good increases of inbound tourism have also been registered by Thailand and Vietnam. However, the impact of the Bali tragedy on the region's tourism remains to be seen.

Elsewhere in the developing world, only South Africa and Central America and perhaps the Caribbean are expecting slight increases of inbound tourism in 2002 over 2001's level. The USA has been one of the source markets hardest hit by all crisis factors together: the events of 11 September 2001, the continuing threat of terrorism in 2002 and the economic recession. Outbound trip volume fell by 12% in the first half of 2002. US outbound travel demand expressed in terms of total spending is forecast to fall by a relatively modest 2% for the full 12 months of 2002, after a decrease of 5% in 2001. As a destination, the Americas overall are expected to still suffer a 6% drop in demand in 2002.

Some general estimates anticipate for 2003 a slight growth of tourism worldwide of up to 2 per cent. A strong growth of 4 per cent or more is predicted for 2004. Such forecasts seem to have the unanimous support of the specialist community, but the risks are also clear: they depend on the absence of further terrorist attacks; more selective reactions by consumers who should not stop travelling altogether when security threats in fact are limited to a location; the development of the conflict in the Middle East and its oil price implications; and last not least on the general prospects of disposable income. In any case, forecasts by renowned specialists and organizations seem to be highly insecure.

Due to the continuing weakness of the world economy, travel and tourism demand in 2003 is likely to be substantially slower than projected earlier, with business travel in particular hit hard by the pressures on companies to cut costs and bolster their profitability. International visitor spending is now expected to recover by a modest 1.6% in 2003 after falling 10% over the previous two years, leaving international visitor spending in 2003 more than 20% below what might have been expected if it had grown by a more typical 5% a year since 2001.

For foreign tourist arrivals to certain European countries in the years to come, forecasts indicate different growth rates. Austria will remain at a modest 2 per cent growth of foreign leisure trip arrivals in 2003. A modest turnaround, with growth of 2% to 3% is expected for the next 12 months also in Germany. In France, international arrivals are expected for 2004 to be back to the pre-2001 growth rate of over 4 per cent, albeit under the assumption that long haul tourism to France will recover. Foreign visitors to Italy in 2003 are expected to increase by 2.7%, making a total of 39 million. Likewise, a growth rate between 2 and 5 per cent is assumed for the near future in Spain.

For the USA, the expectations of the Travel Industry Association of America concerning the growth of international visitor arrivals and expenditures in the years to come. They appear rather optimistic as far as the expenditures are concerned. Forecasts for Canada's foreign tourist arrivals see a growth of 3 per cent each in 2003 and 2004, but astonishingly a slowing down from 2005 on.

A car bomb outside a nightclub in the popular resort of Kuta Beach in Bali (Indonesia) killing almost 200 and injuring over 300 could have had a major effect on the international tourism industry, as tourists were targeted specifically. In any event, the terrorist attack will bear on the performance of the industry in the region of South East Asia and the Pacific, the only region still experiencing strong growth in its tourism flows after September 11, 2002. Probably, the whole region will be affected, as experience shows that tourists' and tour operators' decisions and preferences reflect rather superficial perception of geographical locations and of cultural profiles of destinations.

Bali and with it the whole of Indonesia will suffer badly from the effects of the attack, whereas the impact on other countries in Asia is more difficult to anticipate, as especially East Asia and the Pacific had been experiencing strong growth in spite of the global tourism crisis of 2001. In addition, Asia's tourism more and more relies on growing intra-regional and domestic tourism which, hopefully, will be affected less by the Bali event less than was transatlantic travel after September 11 th , 2001.

Indonesia's inbound tourism had done well in the years following the economic crisis of 1997-8 which it overcame as early as 1999 in terms of tourist arrivals. Receipts from international tourism, however, remained in 1999 (the latest available figure) as much as 25 per cent short of what they were in 1996, which indicates cheaper tourist arrangements or shorter stays per arrival. In 2001, the whole region of East

Asia and the Pacific was little affected by the impact on tourism of the events of 11 September: due to a high growth rate in arrivals before September 11, the region still closed the year with a growth of 5.5 per cent.

Estimates indicate that immediately after the attack of 12 October, Bali's tourism industry virtually collapsed: Airlines cancelled and rerouted a number of their scheduled flights; tourists went home or left to other nearby destinations such as Fiji and the Philippines. As a result, hotel occupation rates tumbled from a comfortable 70 per cent to less than ten per cent. In absolute terms, it can be estimated that from an average of 100,000 tourists present in Bali at any time, not more than 15,000 stayed on. Moreover, it can be assumed that the tourists who stayed on were of Indonesian origin as they represent 15 per cent of all visitors to Bali, and those who left were foreign tourists, leaving behind a devastated tourism economy, especially as far as foreign exchange is concerned. An estimated 5.1 million tourists visited Indonesia in 2001, contributing 5.3 billion dollars to Indonesia's balance of payments (about 9.2 % of total exports). Most of these tourists appear to end up in Bali at one stage or other.

Bali's Minister for Culture and Tourism estimates that the island's tourism economy employed a portion of 65 per cent of the total labour force, i.e. 1,1 million out of the 1.71 million people in employment in Bali with a resident population of 3 million. The hotel and restaurant sector alone produced in 2000 a share of 21 per cent of Real GDP and probably employed an even higher share of the labour force. An estimated drop of 80 per cent in tourism activities would therefore put a total number of close to 300,000 people out of employment in the hotel and restaurant sector, and three times as many in the whole tourism economy including the supply sectors. It can only be hoped that the first wave of tourist cancellations will be overcome before it destroys the jobs irretrievably.

As Bali is considered a magnet for tourists to come to Indonesia and also visit several other parts of the country, the Minister for Culture and Tourism estimates that as many as 2.7 million people may be out of their jobs across Indonesia soon if tourism does not recover quickly. He said that Tourism employed more than seven million people in the South East Asian archipelago and last year brought in 4.7 billion dollars in revenue, or about 10 percent of Indonesia's gross national product (GNP).

Due to slower economic growth and to extra public spending to promote tourism after the Bali bomb attack, Indonesia's public finances will slide deeper into the red, by about 1.5 per cent of gross domestic product next year, up from an earlier projection of 1.3 per cent. The Indonesian economy is now forecasted to expand by just 3.5 to 4 per cent in 2003, down from an earlier estimate of 5 per cent. Prospects to overcome the crisis are not so bad, though, if the steady high growth of international tourism to countries of the region is taken into account. Asia was the only region in the world that maintained strong, albeit uneven growth in tourism during the difficult period after its economic crisis 1997- 98.

A great deal is due to the growth of intra-regional tourism in Asia. During 2001, around 65% of international visitor arrivals in both North East Asia and South East Asia came from within the north eastern plus south eastern Asian region. Prospects of intra-regional Asian tourism count in that from China a total of seven million people travelled overseas in the first half of 2002. The main markets for Indonesian tourism, however, are still Japan and Australia, where Indonesia will make special marketing efforts to counteract the tourism break down after the Bali bombing.

Budget tourists from neighbouring countries like Singapore and Malaysia, as well as many domestic visitors from Indonesia's main island of Java, are replacing tourists from Japan, Australia, and Western markets. Until the end of 2002, their presence largely prevented major layoffs in Bali's tourism industry to occur. But the changing face of Bali tourism means the average visitor stays for a shorter time and spends much less than before-less than half, according to some estimates. Rooms were available in package tours for as little as 25 US Dollars a night. The discounts mean that the income of workers employed in Bali's tourism industry will get squeezed, even if job losses remain modest.

The terrorist attack in Bali will also have a negative impact on the outbound tourism economy of Australia and put a number of Bali travel specialists in Australia out of business. Bali and other islands in the Indonesian archipelago are popular and cheap destinations for Australian families, backpackers and surfers. According to the Australian Bureau of Statistics, in the seven months to July 2002, 144,400 Australians visited Indonesia, amounting to 7.5 percent of outbound tourists.

The Asian region may suffer from indirect effects of the bombing in Bali unnecessarily. This concern was expressed by the Association of South East Asian Nations (ASEAN) when it rejected warnings and advice issued by Western countries including the United States, Britain, Australia and Japan. Such advice had covered all of south east Asia, where tourism accounted for 10.8 percent of GDP and 8.2 percent of employment last year.

The Negative Impact of the Crisis

National tourist authorities and tourist boards, as well as the tourism industry itself - at local and national levels - have reacted in a number of ways. One way, for example, has been to make their destinations more attractive to customers. In many cases, special committees were set up to deal with the situation after September 11th . Partnerships were established between the private sector and public authorities to tackle problems of financial bottlenecks, e.g. the funding of marketing campaigns or the prevention of bankruptcies in the sector. The measures taken range from price reductions introduced by individual enterprises in the areas of travel, hospitality, tour operating, culture and recreation, to large-scale advertising campaigns by tourist authorities. These have often depended upon substantial injections of finance by both the industry and governments.

Advertising campaigns strongly address the domestic tourism markets. For instance, a campaign run by the Travel Industry Association of America (TIA) features the slogan "See America." A comprehensive plan of action was developed by the Travel Industry Association of America to enable the industry and government to work together to reassure the public that travel is safe while rebuilding consumer confidence in travelling both to and within the United States. The USA Small Business Association (SBA) approved a total of US$21.6 million on disaster loans for small travel agencies. The average loan size was US$50,579. One of the reasons was that SBA recognized the hardships facing travel agencies nationwide in the rapidly changing travel market, especially after September 11 th . The SBA also recognized that travel agencies were dramatically affected by reduced airline commissions and advances in technology, specifically the use of the Internet.

A campaign by the Canadian Tourism Commission (CTC) invited Canadians and near-border Americans to re-discover or discover Canada. In fact, the Canadian Government has been supporting a massive marketing campaign by contributing the equivalent of US$13 million to help the hotel industry recover from a loss of US$3.5 billion incurred in 2001.

Austria also ran a major campaign to attract European tourists to their winter sports resorts aimed at replacing missing overseas visitors. One of the most impressive programmes to boost tourism is being developed in the United Kingdom. To overcome the country's deep crisis in international tourism, the British Government and a number of British tourist industry organizations have announced they will back a new international campaign, boosting marketing support for the British tourist industry to the tune of £ 40 million. The government will provide up to £20 million for this new initiative addressed to seven main market countries and aiming to recover at least half of the estimated £2 billion lost by the tourism industry last year. The campaign features over 1,000 special offers put together by both big and small companies throughout the industry, giving discounts of sometimes as much as 50 per cent.

The New Zealand government announced that it is to make US$2.5 million available for the expansion of New Zealand's official tourism classification and quality-grading company, Qualmark, in order to help attract more tourists through improved quality of services. Another example of government support is that of India where, among other relief measures implemented, a 10 per cent expenditure tax on all food and beverages served by hotels was lifted in federal budget announcements in the spring if this year.

In Japan, the government is providing financial support to the troubled travel industry, of which 99 per cent consists of small and medium-sized enterprises. The government's credit association is doubling the maximum loan guarantee for tourism enterprises and government-affiliated financial institutions are doubling the ceiling for unsecured loans.

In general, the tourism sector has been given increased attention by public authorities as a result of the 2001-2002 crisis. Even in southern Europe, which did comparatively well immediately after the September 11 th , both State authorities and the public were sensitized by the crisis and initiatives for private-public partnership increased. One example is a special Euro-Mediterranean group that has been set up on the initiative of Spain and Tunisia to encourage tourism cooperation between the countries of the European Union and Northern Africa.

The industry's endeavours to cut costs, however, strongly affect employment. For example, in a ranking of the 12 types of measures practised most frequently by the US lodging industry to reduce costs, staff reductions and the reduction of working hours are at the top of the list. Six of the first seven measures listed affect staff directly, not to mention any indirect effects from other business reductions.

It is not just ordinary staff but also managers that are losing benefits. Management incentives are predicted to reach only 0.3 per cent of revenues in 2002, or 80.6 per cent less than in 2000, the peak year. In a number of countries, some measures as described above have already been taken. Others will need more time to develop.

The ILO has monitored the developments in the industry with particular emphasis on human resources development, because it was recognized that information on the employment effect of the crisis is still scarce. There is also a need to find more examples of positive action taken by enterprises, social partners and governments aimed at mitigating the impact of the crisis on employment and working conditions. Furthermore, improved methods of measuring the impact on employment of developments in tourism, as well as a series of case studies on good practices, will help to strengthen the capacity of the tourism sector to handle human resources challenges both in normal times and in times of crisis.

In cooperation with different partners, the ILO is prepared to assist developing countries in the modernization of their training systems in the tourism sector in order to help reduce their vulnerability to increased international competition. Raising the quality of services is one possible way of helping to rebuild tourists' confidence after a crisis and it might also have a chance of increasing customer loyalty to a particular destination. As discussed earlier, however, one of the special characteristics of tourism is that customers are able to react quickly to any perception of even a relatively small security risk, because they can easily adjust their plans or make savings if they need to. These reactions can have a significant effect on a country's revenue from tourism in a very short period of time.

The ILO is developing a Tourism Labour Accounts System which is a methodology to measure employment and working conditions in the tourism sector. It will help interested member states to collect and analyse relevant labour data on a continuous basis and in connection with the Tourism Satellite Accounts whose methodology was approved by the United Nations Statistical Commission in 2000. The ILO will continue posting information about developments in employment and working conditions in the Hotel, Catering and Tourism sector as far the data presently available permit.

CHALLENGES

One of the biggest challenges for hotel operations has been the inability to integrate systems. Traditionally, there have been very few interface and integration standards for hotel technology providers. In addition, the notion of making one system work with another has too often been an afterthought. With more and more hoteliers looking to improve guest loyalty and help the bottom line through technology purchases, the complexity - and cost - is compounded. In other words, linking various hotel software systems, at the center of which traditionally lies the PMS (Property Management System), often adds to a hotel's business challenges rather than resolves them, as technology is meant to do.

The problems become exponentially more acute with the advent of so many new Internet sales channels. How does one get all those reservations, now originating in another system, to automatically find their way into my CRS (Central Reservation System) and/or PMS? It is impossible to truly improve yields with a product that expires every night and no centralized inventory to manage.

Interfacing

Interfacing simply describes the notion of one information system delivering or exchanging data with one or more other system. The most basic types of interfaces are often referred to as "device level" interfaces. They are often implemented via a physical cable known as a "serial" connection. Usually they enable a "one-way" data transfer in which, say, a Call Accounting System would send a guest's telephone charges across the interface to the PMS for automatic posting to the guest folio.

Though a basic acknowledgement of message receipt is often part of the interfacing protocol, it is considered by most to be a one-way interface. Other one-way interfaces similarly capture ancillary guest revenue such as Point of Sale charges to the guest folio or enable basic guest services such as the PMS turning on guest-room voice mail upon check-in. Two-way interfaces represent a full exchange of data resulting in an update to the system database at either end. These types of interfaces are usually referred to as "system level" interfaces and are connected from one network to another via FTP or other means.

One common example is the interface between the PMS and a CRS. Reservations taken at a Call Center naturally affect central inventory. The CRS interface sends the reservation information to the PMS whose inventory is now also updated accordingly. Conversely, a walk-in at the property must be made known to the CRS so that it can be updated accordingly. Even beyond this bi-directional reservation flow, greater complexity can be added by sending rate and availability updates from the property to the CRS. Other examples of complex, two-way interfaces are those between a Revenue Management System and a PMS/CRS, or between a PMS and a Sales and Catering system.

Integration

Again, in almost every case where two systems are

interfaced, one or more separate databases are being updated. By most definitions, the notion of integration implies use of only one database or a transactional management system with real time updates. Software services that were traditionally the function of two separate or disparate systems communicating with one another are now engineered into one "single" system. Most examples of integration are found in the area of "system level" software, as opposed to "device level". Though examples are fewer, they do exist. A handful of systems, combine the CRS and PMS around one database or data structure. That way, updates are made in one place only and are thus instantaneous.

The Central Reservation office is working with the same uniform database as the property system(s) so inventory updates are real time. Other examples of integrated systems include resort systems where, for example, the spa management, tee time management and PMS all work from one, uniform database to the point where a stay cancellation inherently cancels a tee time and a spa appointment. Some single providers offer the same net result however, technically speaking, they interface the various system components. If interfacing versus integration is important to you, then ask your provider for the technical explanation.

There is good news for both interfacing and integration. More and more, hotel technology providers in the "device" arena can communicate via means other than serial connections. TCP/IP or other network protocols can be used to effect data transfer or data exchange between two systems. In some cases suppliers have simply re-tooled to offer and adhere to more modern communication protocols. In other cases, providers new to the scene have had the advantage of starting from scratch with newer technologies and, in fact, can only communicate via these new means.

Industry committees such as HTNG (Hotel Technology - Next Generation) are instrumental in representing hoteliers by helping foment change and calling for cooperation among the vendors in the form of standards that ultimately reduce integration costs. In the area of system level interfacing, again, new protocols and new technologies are available. In this case, another industry committee called the OTA (Open Travel Alliance) has adopted a communication language called XML (Extensible Markup Language) as the basis for its eponymous messaging standard.

The OTA specification provides a super-set of pre-defined XML-based message formats, some combination of which are typically interwoven within a product's general communication guidelines to create a usable specification. Previously closed, or proprietary, specifications that cost so much to customize for every new interfaced system, can now take advantage of this open standard.

Perhaps the biggest integration challenge affecting hoteliers top line revenue today is how to maintain and/or synchronize inventory, which now finds itself in so many locations. Hoteliers have to manage Internet Distribution and Global Distribution (Travel Agents) as well as their own proprietary Web portal and call center. True single image inventory is finally arriving with the ability to manage all of the disparate channels through one single user interface.

Integrated Applications and External Systems

Hotels are also requiring unified customer touch points where customers can be recognized at all areas of the enterprise, whether at the front desk, pool, golf course, other property or calling in to their reservation center. True integration enables the customer data to be available within any area of service dramatically improving guest satisfaction and ultimately guest loyalty. These two issues are being addressed by a limited number of solution providers that are focused on true integration. The role of hospitality technology providers has to be redefined in order to answer all of today's integration issues. With organizations such as HTNG, standards such as OTA and providers focused on integration, achieving the ultimate goal of recognizing the guest at every touch point and having true single image inventory is finally possible and will enable lodging companies to succeed in integrating their systems, centralizing their operation and ultimately improving their profitability.

2 Housekeeping Management

Housekeepers run the domestic department/ accommodation services in hotels, guest houses, holiday centres, colleges, and residential homes, among others. This career involves checking that standards of hygiene and maintenance are kept. In order to accomplish this he/she liaises with the different departments within an organisation eg. reception, management, cleaning and maintenance staff.

He/She will take charge of such things as the duty rotas, supervision of work, and ensuring that the necessary equipment is available for staff to carry out their jobs. The training of new staff may also be organised by the housekeeper. Depending on seniority, management may consult with the housekeeper on issues like decoration and furnishings. The housekeeper will often have cleaning duties themselves, particularly in smaller organisations.

Technically no qualifications are required to enter into this career. The specifics of the job may be learned during employment. However there are a variety of courses available which will enable the candidate to enter the profession at a higher level. Some of these courses will require the candidate to have passed five subjects in their

Leaving Certificate. A student on such a course could expect to study subjects such as Housekeeping Management, Hospitality Management, Hospitality Supervision, Hospitality Sales and Marketing, Hospitality Accounting, Guest and Employee Safety, Guest Relations and Care of Cleaning Equipment.

Depending on the educational background of the candidate they may begin their careers cleaning rooms, ensuring guests are comfortable and perhaps room service, depending on the size of the hotel. If the hotel is of a medium or large size there may be opportunities to move into supervisory roles or indeed management. In this case many housekeepers would complete a further course of study in the area of Hotel and Catering Management.

The hotel industry is notorious for long working hours and this area is no exception. A shift in housekeeping could start as early as 5.30am. The working week will not always be Monday to Friday as often the weekends are a hotel's busiest times.

The work can also be physically difficult - carrying heavy cleaning equipment, moving furniture, constantly on one's feet. The job may involve meeting a variety of people and dealing with guests on a one to one level so the development of good interpersonal skills will be an advantage.

The housekeeper will usually develop good managerial skills in order to deal with other staff members and customers in a range of situations. Depending on the seniority of the position the housekeeper may have to manage budgets so a degree of numeracy and accounting ability in this regard will be developed.

The major concern of direction and management of hospital housekeeping programs is the maintenance of environmental sanitation within acceptable levels of bacteriological, as well as visual, cleanliness. The following types of work are come under such programmes:

1. Housekeeping program management in institutions or establishments other than hospitals.
2. Hospital environmental sanitation work which requires full scientific or professional education. Such positions are classified to the appropriate scientific, engineering, or professional subject-matter series.
3. Hospital building management work principally concerned with maintenance and operation of the physical plant.
4. Positions that primarily involve supervision or performance of work for which the paramount requirements are skill and knowledge in the application of hospital housekeeping techniques rather than ability to manage a comprehensive hospital housekeeping program.

Accordingly, hospital housekeeping supervisory positions whose paramount requirement is trade, craft, or laboring experience and knowledge are exempt from the General Schedule and excluded from this series. Such supervisory positions are excluded even though they may operate through subordinate supervisors. In contrast, hospital housekeeping positions whose paramount requirement is knowledge of hospital housekeeping techniques and management procedure, techniques, methods, and practices needed to effectively plan, organize, conduct, and manage a hospital housekeeping program are covered by the General Schedule and included in this series.

The distinction between hospital housekeeping positions which are covered by the General Schedule and those which are excluded is, however, sometimes difficult to make. Hospital housekeeping management and supervisory positions that are under the General Schedule because of a paramount requirement for knowledges and experience related to "management" rather than to trades and crafts may, nevertheless, include a secondary requirement for such trades, craft or laboring experience and knowledge. Conversely, supervisory hospital housekeeping positions which are exempt from the General Schedule because of a paramount requirement for trades, craft, and manual laboring experience and knowledge, may include a secondary requirement for managerial skills similar to those of managers and supervisors under the General Schedule.

Determination of the pay category of a hospital housekeeping position therefore must be based on a careful assessment of the paramount requirement of the position, i.e., does the position primarily require managerial knowledges and skills, or are trade, craft, or manual laboring experience and knowledge the paramount requirement for supervising or directing the involved hospital housekeeping work operations.

For example, fully operational Hospital Housekeeping Officer positions which have the full range of managerial responsibility. Assistant Hospital Housekeeping Officers reporting to Hospital Housekeeping Officers with full managerial responsibility are also covered by the General Schedule when they share in these managerial responsibilities to such an extent that they are the basis for the paramount requirement of the position. On the other hand, supervisory positions reporting directly to Hospital

Housekeeping Officers are exempt from the General Schedule when the performance of supervisory duties, such as planning, scheduling, assigning, coordinating, directing, or reviewing work activities, is primarily based on the application of trade, craft, or manual laboring experience and knowledge rather than on management experience and knowledge of management methods and techniques.

Usually, a careful assessment of the paramount requirement of a position will be sufficient to determine its pay category. Only after such a careful assessment has been inconclusive, may a position be considered to be borderline with respect to pay category. However, in borderline situations, the total working environment of the position, such as the nature of the work organization, working and pay relationships, normal career progression, and management intent must be considered. In this connection, the following should be noted:

Line of Promotion: The overall pattern of past and anticipated career progression is an indicator of whether a position is GS or non-GS. For example, positions in career ladders, or part of a planned program of training, leading to a specific "target" position are in the same pay category as the target position.

Management Intent: The intent of management in establishing a particular hospital housekeeping position is an important indicator to be considered in making the pay category determination for borderline positions. The management "intent" to be considered refers to the manner in which management intends the responsibilities of the position to be exercised, the overall approach to the work involved and the nature of the knowledges and abilities which are to be the basis for carrying out the primary duties of the position. For the purpose of making pay category determinations, management "intent" may be considered to the extent that it is consistent with and reflected by the overall pattern of past and anticipated career progression, and supported by the content of the applicable official position description.

The need for maintaining bacteriological, as well as visual, cleanliness in hospitals has been recognized for some time. However, in recent years, the need to maintain exceptionally high-levels of environmental sanitation has become even more critical. This increasing awareness of the need to maintain a safe and sanitary environment for hospital patients, staff and visitors, culminated in the issuance by the Joint Commission on Accreditation of Hospitals (JCAH) of new and demanding standards of excellence in hospital sanitation. Additionally, new and more stringent requirements for effective occupational safety and health have created increased demands for controlling the physical facilities and the actions of individuals so as to minimize patient, employee or visitor injury and exposure to infectious disease.

As the concern for the hospital environment has evolved to its present level, so too has the position of Hospital Housekeeping Officer evolved to meet the increased demands. At one time, responsibility for maintaining the hospital environment was diffused, with the nursing department assuming considerable responsibility in this area. Later, hospital housekeeping responsibility was centralized in Hospital Housekeeping Officer positions which focused on directing the day-to-day operations of the housekeeping program.

More recently, the new emphasis on hospital sanitation has made it necessary to endow Hospital Housekeeping Officer positions with the full range of managerial responsibilities typical of other administrative managers in hospitals. While the Hospital Housekeeping Officer is still expected to be a technical expert in environmental sanitation and hospital housekeeping, the primary responsibility of these positions has shifted from technical program direction to overall program management and accountability. Today's Hospital Housekeeping Officer has full administrative and managerial responsibility for the environmental sanitation program. Hospital Housekeeping Officers usually report directly to top hospital management (typically the Assistant Hospital Administrator), but this may not be the case in every institution.

The Hospital Housekeeping Officer is fully responsible for planning, organizing, staffing, directing, controlling and evaluating the program at their specific health care facility. They coordinate hospital housekeeping activities with other programs and activities in the hospital; initiate, shape and set policy, procedures, standards and goals; develop and apply an internal program of management review, appraisal and improvement; establish the balance between quality and quantity in light of budget and ceiling constraints; provide for formal and on-the-job training and instruction; and, assume an active role in the overall management responsibility for a health care facility through participation and service in the committee structure.

Hospital Housekeeping Officers formulate, implement, coordinate and control comprehensive environmental sanitation programs. They respond to the myriad components of the health care environment and have the administrative authority to use discretion in effecting needed change for the benefit of patients, staff and visitors. The technical aspects of the Hospital Housekeeping Officer position revolve around the development and maintenance of standards for cleanliness and sanitation. These standards encompass such areas as the frequency of cleaning; the methods, procedures and safety precautions to be followed; the selection, measurement and proper use of housekeeping and cleaning supplies; and the use and maintenance of housekeeping equipment.

In developing standards to meet the unique requirements of a particular hospital, the Hospital Housekeeping Officer must take into consideration both the unique physical characteristics of the local hospital and the functions of various specialized hospital departments and medical programs. Maintaining these standards involves such activities as continuing inspections by the Hospital Housekeeping Officer and subordinate supervisors; a bacteriological monitoring program including the systematic collection, incubation and analysis of sample micro-organism cultures; and an aggressive program to test and perfect hospital housekeeping techniques, procedures and products.

Hospital Housekeeping Officer positions require both technical expertise in hospital housekeeping operations and program management ability. A number of these qualification requirements are mentioned or implied in the preceding occupational information section and the remainder of this standard. The following is not all inclusive, but it does summarize the more important knowledges, skills and abilities required for hospital housekeeping management positions:

— ability to develop procedures which mesh the specific goals of the hospital housekeeping department with the broad overall goals of the hospital, and ability to work with other hospital managers to coordinate respective programs;

— ability to delegate authority;

— ability to analyze problems and make decisions taking into full consideration a wide range of factors and requirements, e.g., standards of the Joint Commission on Accreditation of Hospitals, budgetary and ceiling restrictions, public relations, labor relations, EEO, etc.;

— ability to communicate effectively with a wide variety of people, e.g., justifying program goals and plans to top hospital managers and motivating hospital housekeeping employees;

— familiarity with government-wide, agency, and hospital rules and regulations in areas such as budget, personnel and labor relations, and ability to develop operating procedures for implementing these requirements in the local hospital housekeeping program;.

— practical working knowledge of some of the basic principles of chemistry, biology and bacteriology as applied to environmental sanitation, infection control, and choice and use of cleaning agents and equipment, and as gained by on-the-job training supplemented by related experience, education or special outside courses;

— knowledge of hospital housekeeping methods and techniques; of various floor, wall, and ceiling covering materials and their properties; and of current developments concerning new cleaning agents, techniques and equipment.

These and related qualification requirements have been taken into consideration in establishing the grade structure and are reflected in the grade-level criteria.

Trainees receive systematic hospital classroom and on-the-job training in all major facets of the housekeeping program. Instruction and assignments provide a basic familiarity with hospital objectives and procedures, departmental relationships, and especially with hospital housekeeping objectives, practices, and procedures. The training typically provides indoctrination in management philosophy and supervisory techniques, as well as actual experience in supervising workers, assigning work, establishing schedules, establishing performance standards, and conducting studies to determine whether changes in procedures should be made.

Trainees gain experience in specific techniques for such things as various types of cleaning, linen contrcl and management, laundry operation, interior decoration, testing new products or equipment, and monitoring the level of a bacteriological cleanliness by coordinating or performing culture sampling. All work is performed under close supervision, with detailed instructions provided for specific assignments, and additional guidance given during the course of assignments as necessary.

Work is evaluated both for technical accuracy and as an indicator of ability to grasp and successfully apply basic hospital housekeeping principles and practices, ability to exercise initiative and assume responsibility, and potential for successfully performing more responsible hospital housekeeping management work.

With general instructions as to objectives, priorities and deadlines, the Hospital Housekeeping Assistant uses initiative in planning and carrying out assignments which are covered by instructions, policies, previous training or accepted pracork is reviewed in terms of the adequacy of methods, procedures, recommendations and results; and as an indicator of ability to grasp and solve new and changing problems, effectively deal with hospital housekeeping employees, coordinate hospital housekeeping activities with other hospital departments and potential for successfully performing more responsible hospital housekeeping work.

Characteristics of Programme

Hospital Housekeeping Officer is fully responsible and accountable for planning, directing and monitoring all aspects of the hospital housekeeping program. This includes responsibility for performing the full range of the following duties and responsibilities:

— Determining long-range, intermediate, and short-range program goals and policies independently or jointly with higher management and/or the appropriate hospital committee(s);

— Developing and implementing organizational structures and operating plans and procedures to achieve program goals, monitoring effectiveness and efficiency of operations within the established framework, and making adjustments as necessary;

— Determining need for and allocation of resources, and accounting for their effective use;

— Considering a broad spectrum of factors when making decisions (or recommendations to higher-level management) including requirements of the Joint Commission on Accreditation of Hospitals and the Occupational Safety and Health Administration, public relations, effect on other hospital activities, economic impact, etc.;

— Coordinating program efforts with other internal activities, and, as necessary, program management officials at the headquarters level;

- Understanding agency and local hospital policies and priorities and communicating them throughout the hospital housekeeping department; and communicating the goals of the housekeeping program to other hospital departments;
- Establishing personnel management policies for the housekeeping department which are in line with the general personnel policies of the agency and the local hospital; dealing with personnel actions affecting key employees and with other actions with possible serious repercussions; and
- Delegating authority to subordinate supervisors and holding them responsible for the performance of their respective organizational units.

Positions which fully meet this level of managerial responsibility are to be evaluated in terms of two classification factors: (1) Scope of Program and (2) Hospital Characteristics. The Assistant who serves as a full deputy to the Housekeeping Officer, substantially sharing all technical and managerial responsibilities, may be classified one grade lower than the Hospital Housekeeping Officer. The cleaning function is the nucleus of all hospital housekeeping programs and the prime responsibility of all Hospital Housekeeping Officers. Beyond this, however, some Hospital Housekeeping Officers are also responsible for the management of additional functional areas which significantly increase the complexity of their work.

Additional functional areas complicate the Housekeeping Officer's position when they demand (1) specialized technical knowledges not directly related to basic cleaning operations and (2) increased management skill. At this level the Hospital Housekeeping Officer may also have administrative management responsibility for a variety of incidental functions in addition to basic operations. These incidental functions add to the variety of the program. They do not, however, significantly increase the overall complexity of the Hospital Housekeeping Officer position since (1) they do not require additional specialized knowledges, and (2) they do not generate significant management problems because they are covered by relatively standardized and established requirements, methods and procedures.

In determining whether the Hospital Housekeeping Officer position is to be evaluated at this level, the emphasis must be on the impact the additional functional areas actually have on the position. Positions which involve marginal responsibility for potentially substantive functional areas should not be assigned to this level. The following examples illustrate the degree of responsibility the Hospital Housekeeping Officer must exercise over various substantive functional areas to receive credit at this level. Other functional areas may also be credited if they demand comparable specialized technical knowledge and management skills.

Interior Decoration: Responsibility for interior decoration involves a major role for developing a hospital-wide decorating plan that is both conducive to patient well-being and pleasing to visitors and employees. In developing the plan, the durability, clean ability, suitability, expense and aesthetic value of various types of fabrics and furniture must be fully considered. While the preferences of hospital staff are considered in making decorating decisions, the Hospital Housekeeping Officer exercises final authority for selections, subject only to adjustment by top hospital management and/or the hospital's interior decoration committee.

Laundry: Responsibility involves active participation (together with the laundry plant manager who is responsible for day-to-day laundry operation) in managing the technical operations of the laundry. This includes such activities as the selection and use of equipment, establishment of work standards, and development and revision of work flow procedures.

Control of Linen Management: The Hospital Housekeeping Officer is responsible for the full cycle of linen management. This includes determination of the type of linen to be purchased, the quantity necessary to be kept in stock, establishment of quotas for each ward and other using points within the hospital, establishment of transportation methods and systems for both clean and soiled linen, and arrangement for laundering, repair and replacement of linens.

Hospital's Physical Characteristics

This factor measures the impact of the hospital's physical characteristics on the administrative complexity of the Hospital Housekeeping Officer's position. This increased administrative complexity is manifested in areas such as increased complexity of organizational relationships, a greater need for executive skills and abilities in planning, coordinating, controlling and directing program operations and increased occasions for making difficult decisions and resolving substantive problems.

The following list highlights some of the hospital characteristics which have an impact on the administrative complexity of the Hospital Housekeeping Officer position:

— *operating beds:* A traditional indicator of the size and complexity of hospital facilities, the number of operating beds in a hospital has a direct impact on the Hospital Housekeeping Officers position. In general, increased staff and funds are necessary to operate the hospital housekeeping program in larger hospitals, and, concomitant with these increases, are increased problems in managing the additional resources. A larger hospital also tends to bring a larger overall hospital staff and more hospital visitors. This additional congestion complicates coordination and scheduling of cleaning operations.

— *patient turnover:* Patient turnover affects the general tempo of hospital operations, generates more "crises," and results in a need for additional supplies, equipment and personnel. Patient turnover is calculated by dividing the number of discharges for a typical month by the average daily census and multiplying by 100.

— *outpatient activity:* A large volume of outpatient visits creates extra environmental sanitation demands which require additional space, supplies, equipment and staff. The adequacy of the space available for outpatient visits should also be considered here since there are generally additional problems in maintaining congested areas.

— *medical specialty teaching programs:* Both the number of trainees in the hospital and the variety of medical specialities with formal teaching programs affiliated with medical schools affect the complexity of Hospital Housekeeping Manager positions. Such programs require additional office space and teaching areas and contribute to the overall pace of hospital sanitation demands. Human traffic and congestion of facilities also tend to increase in hospitals as the number and type of medical teaching programs increase.

— *medical research:* Medical research impacts on the Hospital Housekeeping Officer position when it requires separate space which substantially increases the amount of space to be cleaned and which creates a need for special cleaning precautions and techniques, special training for cleaning crews, different standards of bacteriological cleanliness and special attention to the scheduling and timing of cleaning activities.

The examples under the following factor level descriptions characterize the kinds of hospital environments which would typically generate administrative and managerial problems representative of a particular level. However, a position should not be mechanically assigned to a level under this factor based on a simple matching of the examples to the operating characteristics of the hospital. Judgment must be used to properly assess the overall impact of the hospital characteristics on the individual Hospital Housekeeping Officer position. It is the impact of the full range of hospital characteristics on the Hospital Housekeeping Officer position, not the intrinsic properties of the characteristics themselves, which is important for level determining purposes.

Three levels of hospital complexity are described under this factor ranging from small hospitals with relatively stable staff and organizational structures to dynamic multi-mission hospitals and centers. Positions which function in environments which do not meet Level C may not involve the full range of managerial responsibilities characteristic of this series and should be carefully assessed to determine whether they are subject to the General Schedule.

Hospital Housekeeping Officer positions which meet the criteria for inclusion in the General Schedule and function in hospitals whose physical characteristics have a limited impact on the position are typically developmental. These positions should be evaluated by comparison to the criteria in this standard and by consideration of the overall career pattern of the position.

The impact of the health care facility's mission and/or physical characteristics on the administrative complexity of the Hospital Housekeeping Officer position is such that a considerable amount of time is devoted to administrative management rather than direct day-to-day supervision over workforce. The number of beds, patients treated, outpatient visits and patient turnover rate have demonstrably affected the position, requiring the Hospital Housekeeping Officer to effectively respond to the needs of the facility. While the organizational structure of hospitals at this level is well established, problems are created in coordinating housekeeping activities with other hospital departments.

There are demands for specialized cleaning requirements as evidenced by the presence of a moderate number of special medical programs and/or a moderate sized research program. At this level the Hospital Housekeeping Officer supervises through other supervisory personnel, usually two or more, including an assistant.

The following examples illustrate some of the types of hospitals found at this level:

(1) This hospital has 900 general medical and surgical beds. The facility is spread out over 53 hectares (130 acres) and is housed in more than 80 buildings. There are 18 medical specialty teaching programs where residencies have been established and 15 special medical programs. Illustrative of these special programs are cardiac catheterization, drug dependence, hemodialysis, intensive care units,

nuclear medicine and pulmonary function units. The substantive research program is conducted in over 836 square meters (9,000 square feet) of space. The hospital treats 12,534 inpatients and there are 111,000 outpatient visits annually. The patient turnover rate is 140%. Total employment exceeds 1,800 personnel. The Hospital Housekeeping Officer is responsible for maintaining 58,435 square meters (629,000 square feet) of space. Approximately 110 employees are required to carry out the housekeeping services of the hospital.

(2) This 500-bed general medical and surgical hospital is part of a large medical-educational complex located adjacent to a large university complex. In this complex, there are 12 general and special purpose hospitals and clinics encompassing schools of medicine, dentistry, optometry, nursing and other education institutions. This highly active teaching hospital has 19 medical specialty teaching programs; there are 11 special medical programs represented in such specialties as cardiac catheterization, hemodialysis, intensive care units and pulmonary function. Through cooperation with the adjacent university, the hospital has developed an extensive and progressively expanding research program which is primarily housed in a four-story building.

Approximately 13,222 patients are treated in the hospital which has a total of 1,380 full and part-time employees. The hospital also has 97,000 outpatient visits and the patient turnover is 292%. The Hospital Housekeeping Officer, with a staff of 60, is responsible for maintaining an area encompassing 30,286 square meters (326,000 square feet).

(3) This hospital consists of two divisions which are approximately 14 kilometers (9 miles) apart. At one division there is a 209-bed general medical and surgical hospital, 723-bed domiciliary section and a 71-bed nursing home care unit. Altogether there are some 41 buildings and structures located on a 88 hectare (217-acre) reservation. Hospital services include surgery, general medicine, neuropsychiatry, radiology, urology, pathology, orthopedics, opthalmology, otorhinolaryngology, physical medicine and rehabilitation, dentistry, and nursing home and domiciliary care. At the other division there is a 566-bed neuropsychiatric hospital plus a 135-bed intermediate care unit.

There are 45 buildings and structures on 35 hectares (87 acres) of land. The two-division hospital employs 1,330 individuals and treats 7,110 patients annually. The patient turnover rate is 55% and the hospital has 55,000 outpatient visits annually. There is one medical specialty teaching program and 6 special medical programs. Specialized treatment programs include an alcoholic treatment unit, drug abuse unit and Vietnam Era veterans unit. Center research activities are carried on in psychology, psychiatric medicine, physical medicine and rehabilitation and biochemistry. The Hospital Housekeeping Officer and staff of 114 full and part-time employees are responsible for maintaining 52,861 square meters (569,000 square feet).

At this level, the impact of the mission and physical characteristics on the administrative complexity of the Hospital Housekeeping Officer position is exceptional. The size of the facility, patients treated, and annual outpatient visits are significantly greater than at the next lower level.

The volume of activity as reflected in facility staffing necessary to carry out the mission, in combination with the rapid rate of patient turnover, has an extraordinary impact on the management of the hospital housekeeping program. At this level, the large number of highly specialized medical and research programs and the variety of medical specialties having residency programs, have a significantly greater impact on the management of the hospital housekeeping program than at the next lower level. The following examples illustrate some of the types of hospitals found at this level:

(1) This 1,330-bed general medical and surgical hospital includes a 78-bed nursing home care unit. There are 59 buildings on approximately 48 hectares (118 acres). The hospital is located within a short distance of a large city and is adjacent to a medical center and a.large college of medicine. The hospital is equipped with the most modern facilities and is very actively affiliated, having 25 medical speciality teaching programs and 15 special medical programs. There is an extensive research program. The 2,834 employees care for 20,812 inpatients and 230,000 outpatient visits annually. The patient turnover rate is 151%. The Hospital Housekeeping Officer, along with a staff of 187 employees, has responsibility for maintaining 88,443 square meters (952,000 square feet) of space.

(2) The Hospital Housekeeping Officer is responsible for a general medical and surgical consolidated facility of approximately 1,000 beds, plus a 100-bed nursing home care unit. The hospital engages in diverse educational affiliations and training programs, a research program and participates in community and comprehensive health planning activities, including agreements to

share specialized medical resources. There are two divisions which are geographically dispersed by a number of kilometers (miles); one division primarily involving one high rise building, is located in the "inner city" and the other in a more rural environment having many buildings spread out over 55 hectares (135 acres). The patient turnover rate exceeds 150%. Over 16,000 inpatients and 200,000 outpatients are treated annually. The hospital is actively affiliated, having between 7 and 11 medical specialties and 15 special medical programs. The Hospital Housekeeping Officer and his staff of 140 employees is responsible for maintaining 46,544 square meters (501,000 square feet) of space which is spread out over 55 hectares (137 acres). Research is conducted in speech pathology, cardiovascular system, hypertension, cancer chemotherapy, atherosclerosis, endocrinology, hematology, aging, pharmacology, rheumatology, surgery and transplantation.

(3) This general medical and surgical hospital center with approximately 1,300 beds includes a 500-bed long-term patient care unit. It is a teaching institution affiliated with a large university, having 15 medical specialty teaching programs and 12 special medical programs. The hospital employs 3,141 full and part-time personnel who care for about 15,000 inpatients; there are about 183,000 outpatient visits per year. The patient turnover rate is 183%. Extensive research programs are ongoing in a number of medical specialities. The Hospital Housekeeping Officer, together with a staff of 284 employees, is responsible for directing an environmental sanitation program for an area that encompasses about 71,163 square meters (766,000 square feet).

3

Staff Management

A comfortable room, good food, and a helpful staff can make being away from home an enjoyable experience for both vacationing families and business travelers. While most lodging managers work in traditional hotels and motels, some work in other lodging establishments, such as camps, inns, boardinghouses, dude ranches, and recreational resorts. In full-service hotels, lodging managers help their guests have a pleasant stay by providing many of the comforts of home, including cable television, fitness equipment, and voice mail, as well as specialized services such as health spas. For business travelers, lodging managers often schedule available meeting rooms and electronic equipment, including slide projectors and fax machines.

Lodging managers are responsible for keeping their establishments efficient and profitable. In a small establishment with a limited staff, the manager may oversee all aspects of operations. However, large hotels may employ hundreds of workers, and the general manager usually is aided by a number of assistant managers assigned to the various departments of the operation. In hotels of every size, managerial duties vary significantly by job title.

General managers, for example, have overall responsibility for the operation of the hotel. Within guidelines established by the owners of the hotel or executives of the hotel chain, the general manager sets room rates, allocates funds to departments, approves expenditures, and establishes expected standards for guest service, decor, housekeeping, food quality, and banquet operations. Managers who work for chains also may organize and staff a newly built hotel, refurbish an older hotel, or reorganize a hotel or motel that is not operating successfully. In order to fill entry-level service and clerical jobs in hotels, some managers attend career fairs.

Resident managers live in hotels and are on call 24 hours a day to resolve problems or emergencies. In general, though, they typically work an 8- to 10 hour day and oversee the day-to-day operations of the hotel. In many hotels, the general manager also is the resident manager. Executive housekeepers ensure that guest rooms, meeting and banquet rooms, and public areas are clean, orderly, and well maintained. They also train, schedule, and supervise the work of housekeepers, inspect rooms, and order cleaning supplies.

Front office managers coordinate reservations and room assignments, as well as train and direct the hotel's front desk staff. They ensure that guests are treated courteously, complaints and problems are resolved, and requests for special services are carried out. Front office managers may adjust charges posted on a customer's bill. Convention services managers coordinate the activities of various departments in larger hotels to accommodate meetings, conventions, and special events. They meet with representatives of groups or organizations to plan the number of rooms to reserve, the desired configuration of the meeting space, and the banquet services. During the meeting or event, they resolve unexpected problems and monitor activities to ensure that hotel operations conform to the expectations of the group.

Assistant managers help run the day-to-day operations of the hotel. In large hotels, they may be responsible for activities such as personnel, accounting, office administration, marketing and sales, purchasing, security, maintenance, and pool, spa, or recreational facilities. In smaller hotels, these duties may be combined into one position. Assistant managers may adjust charges on a hotel guest's bill when a manager is unavailable.

Computers are used extensively by lodging managers and their assistants to keep track of guests' bills, reservations, room assignments, meetings, and special events. In addition, computers are used to order food, beverages, and supplies, as well as to prepare reports for hotel owners and top-level managers. Managers work with computer specialists to ensure that the hotel's computer system functions properly. Should the hotel's computer system fail, managers must continue to meet the needs of hotel guests and staff.

Working Conditions

Because hotels are open around the clock, night and weekend work is common. Many lodging managers work more than 40 hours per week. Managers who live in the hotel usually have regular work schedules, but they may be called to work at any time. Some employees of resort hotels are managers during the busy season and have other duties during the rest of the year.

Lodging managers sometimes experience the pressures of coordinating a wide range of functions. Conventions and large groups of tourists may present unusual problems. Moreover, dealing with irate guests can be stressful. The job can be particularly hectic for front office managers during check-in and check-out time. Computer failures can further complicate an already busy time.

Lodging managers held about 69,000 jobs in 2002. Self-employed managers—primarily owners of small hotels and motels—held about 50 percent of these jobs. Companies that manage hotels and motels under contract employed some managers.

Training and other Qualifications

Hotels increasingly emphasize specialized training. Postsecondary training in hotel or restaurant management is preferred for most hotel management positions, although a college liberal arts degree may be sufficient when coupled with related hotel experience. Internships or part-time or summer work are an asset to students seeking a career in hotel management. The experience gained and the contacts made with employers can greatly benefit students after graduation. Most bachelor's degree programs include work-study opportunities.

Community colleges, junior colleges, and some universities offer associate's, bachelor's, and graduate degree programs in hotel or restaurant management. Combined with technical institutes, vocational and trade schools, and other academic institutions, over 800 educational facilities have programs leading to formal recognition in hotel or restaurant management. Hotel management programs include instruction in hotel administration, accounting, economics, marketing, housekeeping, food service management and catering, and hotel maintenance engineering. Computer training also is an integral part of hotel management training, due to the widespread use of computers in reservations, billing, and housekeeping management. Additionally, over 450 high schools in 45 States offer the Lodging Management Program created by the Educational Institute of the American Hotel and Lodging Association. This is a two-year program offered to high school juniors and seniors, which teaches management principles and leads to a professional certification called the "Certified Rooms Division Specialist". Many colleges and universities grant participants credit towards a post-secondary degree in hotel management.

Lodging managers must be able to get along with many different people, even in stressful situations. They must be able to solve problems and concentrate on details. Initiative, self-discipline, effective communication skills, and the ability to organize and direct the work of others also are essential for managers at all levels. In the past, many managers were promoted from the ranks of front desk clerks, housekeepers, waiters, chefs, and hotel sales workers. Although some employees still advance to hotel management positions without education beyond high school, postsecondary education is preferred.

Restaurant management training or experience also is a good background for entering hotel management, because the success of a hotel's food service and beverage operations often is important to the profitability of the entire establishment. Graduates of hotel or restaurant management programs usually start as trainee assistant managers. Some large hotels sponsor specialized on-the-job management training programs that allow trainees to rotate among various departments and gain a thorough knowledge of the hotel's operation. Other hotels may help finance formal training in hotel management for outstanding employees. Newly built hotels, particularly those without established on-the-job training programs, often prefer to hire applicants who have hotel management experience.

Large hotel and motel chains may offer better opportunities for advancement than small, independently owned establishments, but relocation every several years often is necessary for advancement. The large chains have more extensive career ladder programs and offer managers the opportunity to transfer to another hotel or motel in the chain or to the central office. Career advancement can be accelerated by the completion of certification programs offered by various associations. These programs usually require a combination of course work, examinations, and experience. For example, outstanding lodging managers may advance to higher level manager positions.

Employment of lodging managers is expected to grow more slowly than the average for all occupations through 2012. Additional job openings are expected to occur as experienced managers transfer to other occupations or leave the labor force, in part because of the long hours and stressful working conditions. Job opportunities are expected to be best for persons with college degrees in hotel or restaurant management.

Increasing business travel and domestic and foreign tourism will drive employment growth of lodging managers. Managerial jobs are not expected to grow as rapidly as the hotel industry overall, however. As the industry consolidates, many chains and franchises will acquire independently owned establishments and increase the numbers of economy-class rooms to accommodate bargain-conscious guests. Economy hotels offer clean, comfortable rooms and front desk services without costly extras such as restaurants and room service. Because there are not as many departments in these hotels, fewer managers will be needed. Similarly, the increasing number of extended-stay hotels will temper demand for managers because, in these establishments, management is not required to be available 24 hours a day. In addition, front desk clerks increasingly are assuming some responsibilities previously reserved for managers, further limiting the employment growth of managers and their assistants.

Additional demand for managers is expected in suite hotels, because some guests—especially business customers—are willing to pay higher prices for rooms with kitchens and suites that provide the space needed to conduct meetings. In addition, large full-service hotels—offering restaurants, fitness centers, large meeting rooms, and play areas for children, among other amenities—will continue to provide many trainee and managerial opportunities.

Median annual earnings of lodging managers were $33,970 in 2002. The middle 50 percent earned between $26,110 and $44,670. The lowest 10 percent earned less than $20,400, while the highest 10 percent earned more than $59,420.

Salaries of lodging managers vary greatly according to their responsibilities and the segment of the hotel industry in which they are employed, as well as the location and region where the hotel is located. Managers may earn bonuses of up to 25 percent of their basic salary in some hotels and also may be furnished with lodging, meals, parking, laundry, and other services. In addition to providing typical benefits, some hotels offer profit-sharing plans and educational assistance to their employees. Other occupations concerned with organizing and directing a business in which customer service is the cornerstone of their success include food service managers, gaming managers, sales worker supervisors, and property, real estate, and community association managers.

Role of Food Service Managers

Food is consumed outside the home in a variety of settings. Eating places range from institutional cafeterias and fast food to elegant dining establishments. The cuisine, price, and setting where the meals are consumed vary, but managers of these dining facilities share many of the same responsibilities. Efficient and profitable operation of restaurants and institutional food service facilities requires managers and assistant managers to select and appropriately price menu items, use food and other supplies efficiently, and achieve consistent quality in food preparation and service. They also must attend to the various administrative aspects of the business, which includes recruiting, training, and supervising an adequate number of workers.

In most restaurants and institutional food service facilities, the manager is assisted by one or more assistant managers, depending on the size and operating hours of the establishment. In large establishments, as well as in many smaller ones, the management team consists of a general manager, one or more assistant managers, and an executive chef. The executive chef is responsible for the operation of the kitchen, while the assistant managers oversee service in the dining room and other areas of the operation. In smaller restaurants, the executive chef may be the general manager, and sometimes an owner. In fast-food restaurants and other food service facilities open for long hours or 7 days a week, the manager is aided by several assistant .

Many restaurants rarely change their menu, while others make frequent alterations. Institutional food service facilities and some restaurants offer a new menu every day. Managers or executive chefs select menu items, taking into account the likely number of customers, and the past popularity of dishes. Other issues taken into consideration when planning a menu include food left over from prior meals that should not be wasted, the need for variety, and the availability of foods due to seasonality and other factors.

Managers or executive chefs analyze the recipes of the dishes to determine food, labor, overhead costs and to assign prices to the various dishes. Menus must be developed far enough in advance that supplies can be ordered and received in time. Ordering supplies and dealing with suppliers are important aspects of the work of restaurant and food service managers. On a daily basis, managers estimate food consumption, place orders with suppliers, and schedule the delivery of fresh food and beverages. They receive and check the content of deliveries, evaluating the quality of meats, poultry, fish, fruits, vegetables, and baked goods.

Managers meet with the sales representatives from restaurant suppliers to place orders replenishing stocks of tableware, linens, paper, cleaning supplies, cooking utensils, and furniture and fixtures. They also arrange for equipment maintenance and repairs, and for a variety of services such as waste removal and pest control. Managers interview, hire, and, when necessary, fire employees. They explain the establishment's policies and practices to newly hired workers and oversee their training. Managers schedule the work hours of employees, making sure there are enough workers present to cover peak dining periods.

Restaurant and food service managers supervise the kitchen and the dining room. They oversee food preparation and cooking, examining the quality and portion sizes to ensure that dishes are prepared and garnished correctly and in a timely manner. They also investigate and resolve customers' complaints about food quality or service. During busy periods, managers "roll up their sleeves" and help with the cooking, clearing of tables, or other tasks. They direct the cleaning of the kitchen and dining areas and the washing of tableware, kitchen utensils, and equipment to maintain company and government sanitation standards. They monitor the actions of their employees and patrons on a continual basis to ensure the health and safety standards and local liquor regulations are obeyed.

Managers have a variety of administrative responsibilities. In larger stablishments, much of this work is delegated to a bookkeeper, but in others, managers must keep accurate records of the hours and wages of employees, prepare the payroll, and do paperwork to comply with licensing laws and reporting requirements of tax, wage and hour, unemployment compensation, and Social Security laws. They also maintain the records of supplies and equipment purchased, and ensure that accounts with suppliers are paid on a regular basis. In addition, managers record the number, type, and cost of items sold to exclude dishes that are unpopular or less profitable.

Many managers are able to ease the burden of record keeping and paperwork through the use of computers. Point-of-service-systems (POS) are used in many restaurants to increase employee productivity and allow managers to track the sales of specific menu items. Using a POS system, a server keys in the customer's order and the computer immediately sends the order to the kitchen so preparation can begin. The same system totals checks, acts as a cash register and credit card authorizer, and tracks daily sales. To minimize food costs and spoilage, many managers use inventory tracking software to compare the record of daily sales from the POS with a record of present inventory.

In some establishments, when supplies needed for the preparation of popular menu items run low, additional inventory can be ordered directly from the supplier using the computer. Managers are among the first to arrive and the last to leave. At the conclusion of each day, or sometimes each shift, managers tally the cash and charge receipts received and balance them against the record of sales. They are responsible for depositing the day's receipts at the bank, or securing it in a safe place. Managers are also responsible for locking up, checking that ovens, grills, and lights are off, and switching on alarm systems.

Evenings and weekends are popular dining periods, making night and weekend work common. However, many managers of institutional food service facilities work more conventional hours because factory and office cafeterias are generally open only on weekdays for breakfast and lunch. It is common for restaurant and food service managers to work 50 hours or more per week. Managers often experience the pressure of simultaneously coordinating a wide range of activities. When problems occur, it is the responsibility of the manager to resolve them with minimal disruption to customers. The job can be hectic during peak dining hours, and dealing with irate customers or uncooperative employees can be stressful.

Restaurant and food service managers held about 526,500 jobs in 1994. Most worked in restaurants or for contract institutional food service companies, but a small number were also employed by educational institutions, hospitals, nursing and personal care facilities, and civic, social, and fraternal organizations. About two-fifths were self-employed. Jobs are located throughout the country, but are most plentiful in large cities and tourist areas.

Many restaurant and food service manager positions are filled by promoting experienced food and beverage preparation and service workers. Waiters, waitresses, chefs, and fast-food workers who have demonstrated their potential for handling increased responsibility sometimes advance to assistant manager or management trainee jobs when openings occur. Executive chefs need extensive experience working as a chef, and general managers need experience working as assistant manager. However, most food service management companies and national or regional restaurant chains also recruit management trainees from 2- and 4-year college hospitality management programs.

Food service and restaurant chains prefer to hire people with degrees in restaurant and institutional food service management, but they often hire graduates with degrees in other fields who have demonstrated interest and aptitude. A bachelor's degree in restaurant and food service management provides a particularly strong preparation for a career in this occupation. In 1992, more than 160 colleges and universities offered 4 -year programs in restaurant and hotel management or institutional food service management. For people not interested in pursing a 4 -year degree, a good alternative is the more than 800 community and junior colleges, technical institutes, and other institutions that offer programs in these fields leading to an associate degree or other formal certification. Both 2 and 4 -year programs provide instruction in subjects such as accounting, business law and management, food planning and preparation, and nutrition. Some programs combine classroom and laboratory study with internships that provide on-the-job experience. In addition, many educational institutions offer culinary programs that provide food preparation training which can lead to a career as a cook or chef and provide a foundation for advancement to an executive chef position.

Most employers emphasize personal qualities. Restaurant and food service management can be demanding, so good health and stamina are important. Self-discipline, initiative, and leadership ability are essential. Managers must be able to solve problems and concentrate on details. They need good communication skills to deal with customers and suppliers, as well as to motivate and direct their subordinates. A neat and clean appearance is a must because they are often in close personal contact with the public.

Most restaurant chains and food service management companies have rigorous training programs for their management positions. Through a combination of classroom and on-the-job training, trainees receive instruction and gain work experience in all aspects of the operations of a restaurant or institutional food service facility-food preparation, nutrition, sanitation, security, company policies and procedures, personnel management, record keeping, and preparation of reports. Usually after 6 months or a year, trainees receive their first permanent assignment as an assistant manager.

A measure of professional achievement for restaurant and food service managers is to earn the designation of certified Foodservice Management Professional (FMP). Although not a requirement for employment or advancement in the occupation, voluntary certification provides recognition of professional competence, particularly for managers who acquired their skills largely on the job. The Educational Foundation of the National Restaurant Association awards the FMP designation to managers who achieve a qualifying score on a written examination, complete a series of courses that cover a range of food service management topics, and who meet standards of work experience in the field.

Willingness to relocate often is essential for advancement to positions with greater responsibility. Managers advance to larger establishments, or regional management positions within restaurant chains. Some eventually open their own eating and drinking establishments. Others transfer to hotel management positions, because their restaurant management experience provides a good background for food and beverage manager jobs at hotels and resorts.

Employment of restaurant and food service managers is expected to increase faster than the average for all occupations through the year 2005. In addition to growth in demand, the need to replace managers who transfer to other occupations or stop working will create many job openings. Job opportunities are expected to be best for people with bachelor's or associate degrees in restaurant and institutional food service management.

Employment growth is expected to vary by industry. Eating and drinking places will provide the most new jobs as the number of eating and drinking establishments increases and other industries continue to contract out their food services. Population growth, rising personal incomes, and increased leisure time will continue to produce growth in the number of meals consumed outside the home. To meet the demand for prepared food, more restaurants will be built, and more managers will be employed to supervise them. In addition, the number of manager jobs will increase in eating and drinking places as schools, hospitals, and other businesses contract out more of their food services to institutional food service companies located in the eating and drinking industry.

Employment of wage and salary managers in eating and drinking places is expected to increase more rapidly than self-employed managers. New restaurants are increasingly affiliated with national chains rather than being independently owned and operated. As this trend continues, fewer owners will manage restaurants themselves, and more restaurant managers will be employed to run the establishments. Employment in eating and drinking establishments is not very sensitive to changes in economic conditions, so restaurant and food service managers are rarely laid off during hard times. However, competition among restaurants is always intense, and many restaurants do not survive.

Food service manager jobs are expected to increase in other industries, but growth will be slowed as contracting out becomes more common. Growth in the population of elderly people is expected to result in growth of food service manager jobs in nursing homes, residential care facilities, and other health care institutions.

Median earnings for restaurant and food service managers were $421 a week in 1994. The middle 50 percent earned between about $295 and $599 a week. The lowest paid 10 percent earned $220 a week or less, while the highest paid 10 percent earned over $884 a week. Earnings of restaurant and food service managers vary greatly according to their responsibilities and the type and size of establishment. Based on a survey conducted for the National Restaurant Association, the median base salary of managers in restaurants was estimated to be about $28,600 a year in

1994, but managers of the largest restaurants and institutional food service facilities often had annual salaries in excess of $45,000. Managers of fast-food restaurants had an estimated median base salary of $25,000 a year; managers of full-menu restaurants with table service, almost $30,000; and managers of commercial and institutional cafeterias, nearly $31,400 a year in 1994. Besides a salary, most managers received an annual bonus or incentive payment based on their performance. In 1994, most of these payments ranged between $2,000 and $8,000 a year.

Executive chefs had an estimated median base salary of about $37,000 a year in 1994, but those employed in the largest restaurants and institutional food service facilities often had base salaries over $43,000. Annual bonus or incentive payments of most executive chefs ranged between $1,500 and $6,000 a year. The estimated median base salary of assistant managers was over $22,000 a year in 1994, but ranged from less than $19,000 in fast-food restaurants to over $25,000 in some of the largest restaurants and food service facilities. Annual bonus or incentive payments of most assistant managers ranged between $1,000 and $4,000 a year.

Manager trainees had an estimated median base salary of about $20,000 a year in 1994, but had salaries of nearly $30,000 in some of the largest restaurants and food service facilities. Annual bonus or incentive payments of most trainees ranged between $500 and $2,500 a year. Most salaried restaurant and food service managers received free meals, sick leave, health and life insurance, 1 to 3 weeks of paid vacation a year, and the opportunity for additional training depending on their length of service.

Restaurant and food service managers direct the activities of businesses which provide a service to customers. Other managers in service-oriented businesses include hotel managers and assistants, health services administrators, retail store managers, and bank managers.

Information about job opportunities may be obtained from local employers and local offices of the State employment service. Information about a career as a restaurant and food service manager, 2- and 4- year college programs in restaurant and food service management, and certification as a Foodservice Management

A comfortable room, good food, and a helpful hotel staff can make being away from home an enjoyable experience for both vacationing families and business travelers. Hotel managers and assistant managers strive to ensure their guests will have a pleasant stay. Hotel managers are responsible for the efficient and profitable operation of their establishments. In a small hotel, motel, or inn with a limited staff, a single manager may direct all aspects of operations. However, large hotels may employ hundreds of workers, and the general manager may be aided by a number of assistant managers assigned to the various departments of the operation. Assistant managers must ensure that the day-to-day operations of their departments meet the standards set by the general manager.

The general manager has overall responsibility for the operation of the hotel. Within guidelines established by the owners of the hotel or executives of the hotel chain, the general manager sets room rates, allocates funds to departments, approves expenditures, and establishes standards for service to guests, decor, housekeeping, food quality, and banquet operations. Managers who work for chains also may be assigned to organize and staff a newly built hotel, refurbish an older hotel, or reorganize a hotel or motel that is not operating successfully.

Resident managers live in hotels and are on call 24 hours a day to resolve problems or emergencies. However, they typically work an 8-hour day, while overseeing the day-to-day operations of the hotel. In many hotels, the general manager also serves as the resident manager. Executive housekeepers are responsible for ensuring guest rooms, meeting and banquet rooms, and public areas are clean, orderly, and well maintained. They train, schedule, and supervise the work of housekeepers, inspect rooms, and order cleaning supplies.

Front office managers coordinate reservations and room assignments as well as train and direct the hotel's front desk staff. They ensure guests are treated courteously, complaints and problems that may arise are resolved, and requests for special services are carried out. Food and beverage managers direct the food service operations of hotels. They oversee the hotels' restaurants, cocktail lounges, and banquet facilities. They supervise and schedule food and beverage preparation and service workers, plan menus, estimate costs, and deal with food suppliers.

Convention services managers coordinate the activities of large hotels' various departments for meetings, conventions, and special events. They meet with representatives of groups or organizations to plan the number of rooms to reserve, the desired configuration of hotel meeting space, and any banquet services needed. During the meeting or event, they resolve unexpected problems and monitor activities to check that hotel operations conform to the expectations of the group.

Other assistant managers are responsible for personnel, accounting and office administration, marketing and sales, purchasing, security, maintenance, and recreational facilities. Because hotels are open around the clock, night and weekend work is common. Many hotel managers work considerably more than 40 hours per week. Managers who live in the hotel usually have regular work schedules, but they may be called to work at any time. Some employees of resort hotels are managers during the busy season and have other duties during the rest of the year.

Hotel managers sometimes experience the pressures of coordinating a wide range of functions. Conventions and large groups of tourists may present unusual problems. Dealing with irate patrons can be stressful. The job can be particularly hectic for front office managers around check-in and check-out time. Hotel managers and assistant managers held about 105,000 wage and salary jobs in 1994. An additional number-primarily owners of small hotels and motels-were self-employed. Some were employed by companies that manage hotels and motels under contract.

Postsecondary training in hotel or restaurant management is preferred for most hotel management positions, although a college liberal arts degree may be sufficient when coupled with related hotel experience. In the past, most managers were promoted from the ranks of front desk clerks, housekeepers, waiters and chefs, and hotel sales workers. Although some employees still advance to hotel management positions without the benefit of education or training beyond high school, postsecondary education is preferred. Nevertheless, experience working in a hotel-even part time while in school-is an asset to anyone seeking a career in hotel management.

Restaurant management training or experience is also a good background for entering hotel management because the success of a hotel's food service and beverage operations is often of great importance to the profitability of the entire establishment. A bachelor's degree in hotel and restaurant administration provides particularly strong preparation for a career in hotel management. In 1994, over 160 colleges and universities offered bachelor's and graduate programs in this field. Over 800 community and junior colleges, technical institutes, vocational and trade schools, and other academic institutions also have programs leading to an associate degree or other formal recognition in hotel or restaurant management. Graduates of hotel or restaurant management programs usually start as trainee assistant managers, or at least advance to such positions more quickly.

Hotel management programs include instruction in hotel administration, accounting, economics, marketing, housekeeping, food service management and catering, and hotel maintenance engineering. The widespread use of computers in hotel operations such as reservations, accounting, and housekeeping management is making some familiarity with computers essential. Programs encourage part-time or summer work in hotels and restaurants because the experience gained and the contacts made with employers may benefit students when they seek full-time employment after graduation.

Hotel managers must be able to get along with all kinds of people, even in stressful situations. They need initiative, self-discipline, and the ability to organize and direct the work of others. They must be able to solve problems and concentrate on details. Sometimes large hotels sponsor specialized on-the-job management training programs which allow trainees to rotate among various departments and gain a thorough knowledge of the hotel's operation. Other hotels may help finance the necessary training in hotel management for outstanding employees.

Most hotels promote employees who have proven their ability. Newly built hotels, particularly those without well-established on-the-job training programs, often prefer experienced personnel for managerial positions. Large hotel and motel chains may offer better opportunities for advancement than small, independently owned establishments, but relocation every several years often is necessary for advancement. The large chains have more extensive career ladder programs and offer managers the opportunity to transfer to another hotel or motel in the chain or to the central office if an opening occurs. Career advancement can be accelerated by completion of certification programs offered by the associations listed below. These programs generally require a combination of course work, examinations, and experience.

Opportunities to enter hotel management are expected to be good for persons who have college degrees in hotel or restaurant management. Employment of salaried hotel managers is expected to faster than the average for all occupations through the year 2005. Business travel will continue to grow, and increased domestic and foreign tourism will also create demand for additional hotels and motels. However, manager jobs are not expected to grow as rapidly as in the past because an increasing share of the hotel industry will be comprised of economy properties, which generally have fewer managers than full-service hotels.

In the face of financial constraints, guests are becoming more bargain-conscious, and hotel chains are increasing the number of rooms in economy class hotels. Economy hotels offer clean, comfortable rooms and front desk services without costly extras like restaurants and room service. Because there are not as many departments in each hotel, fewer managers are needed on the hotel premises. Economy hotels have a general manager, and regional offices of the hotel management company employ department managers, such as executive housekeepers, to oversee several hotels.

Although new employment growth is expected to be concentrated in economy hotels, large full-service hotels will continue to offer many trainee and managerial opportunities. Most openings are expected to occur as experienced managers transfer to other occupations, retire, or stop working for other reasons.

Salaries of hotel managers vary greatly according to their responsibilities and the segment of the hotel industry in which they are employed. In early 1995, annual salaries of assistant hotel managers averaged nearly $40,000, based on a hospitality industry survey conducted by Roth Young. Salaries of assistant managers also varied because of differences in duties and responsibilities. For example, food and beverage directors averaged $44,000, according to the same survey, whereas front office managers averaged $30,000. The manager's level of experience is also an important factor.

In 1995, salaries of general managers averaged nearly $57,000, according to the Roth Young survey. Their salaries ranged from $40,000 to $81,000 depending on the size and type of establishment. Managers may earn bonuses up to 25 percent of their basic salary in some hotels. In addition, they and their families may be furnished with lodging, meals, parking, laundry, and other services. Most managers and assistants receive 3 to 11 paid holidays a year, paid vacation, sick leave, life insurance, medical benefits, and pension plans. Some hotels offer profit-sharing plans, educational assistance, and other benefits to their employees.

Hotel managers and assistants are not the only workers concerned with organizing and directing a business where customer service is the cornerstone of their success. Other occupations sharing similar responsibilities include restaurant managers, apartment building managers, retail store managers, and office managers.

Tips for aligning human resources with overall organizational strategy Virtually every company can quantify its corporate strategy via income statements and balance sheets, but few are prepared to qualify the extent to which its human assets play a role in its success. New York University research has even suggested that 85 percent of the value of contemporary organizations may be traced to intangible assets—those qualities that cannot easily be defined or classified. As noted by the Society for Human Resource Management, many financially based management systems instead focus on tangible assets and "treat human capital as an expense and not as an asset."

Over the years, those at the highest levels of leadership have come to understand, at least in part, that the corporate "knowledge base" is built on the expertise, talents, and dedication of employees. To understand the role of human capital in business strategy formulation and the extent to which human resources are aligned with organizational strategy, SHRM and the Balanced Scorecard Collaborative surveyed members last fall.

Among other things, the survey sought to understand how organizations describe and manage their corporate strategy. While three-fourths of the survey's 1,310 respondents reported that their organizations have a clearly articulated strategic direction, less than half (44 percent) indicated that their organizations do a good job of communicating that strategy.

Also telling: Two in 10 respondents said that the general employee base understands their company's strategic direction, compared with 89 percent of respondents who reported that the senior management team understands where the company is going. Meanwhile, roughly two-thirds of respondents—primarily HR professionals—reported that they understood their employer's strategic direction.

The SHRM/BSCol Aligning HR with Organization Strategy Survey also reveals that 60 percent of organizations have a formalized strategic planning process, but only 38 percent have a formalized human resources strategic planning process. While 60 percent of survey respondents revealed that HR and overall strategic planning are fully integrated, 13 percent indicated that there is no relationship between the two.

On the subject of human capital, 65 percent of respondents reported that their organizations do not have a consistent way of describing the contributions their employees make. Moreover, only a quarter have a clearly articulated approach for measuring human capital.

Dennis Hatch, corporate director of human resources for Sonesta International Hotels Corporation, confirms that the management of human capital factors heavily into Sonesta's strategic-planning process at all levels. "It starts with knowing what you're all about," says Hatch, a six-year veteran of the Boston, Massachusetts-based hotel management company. (Founded in the 1940s, Sonesta today owns, manages, or licenses 25 hotels and resorts in five countries.) "Sonesta has a clearly delineated purpose and four guiding principles. We talk about them all the time. All employees know what they are because we weave them into training, goal setting, and performance reviews." Those values include practicing "the highest standards of integrity and ethics in the way we conduct our business";

valuing employees as individuals; exceeding customers' expectations; and delivering "service with passion."

Hatch says the company also has done a good job of incorporating the HR function into its overall business philosophy. "All of our HR people are members of the executive committee either at the property level or at headquarters," he explains. "It's not about forcing your way in, but just creating value in what you do. You do that by perpetuating the good things you do and coming up with new ideas. We have recently looked at how we train our managers and do performance reviews. When we do employee climate surveys [which measure how employees feel about certain issues], we ask value questions such as, 'Are your managers honest?' 'Are they treating you with dignity and respect?' We work together to make improvements all the time."

Today nearly all hospitality companies are using job boards as part of their recruitment strategy. These sites have two primary functions for employers: job postings, to which job seekers can apply directly and a resume database, in which employers can search for candidates. While technology and features may differ slightly between websites, there are clear strategies that companies can utilize which will make their internet recruitment process more manageable and will enable them to consistently attract the best talent.

It is important to understand that these two functions will garner two different types of candidates. Individuals who apply to job postings (or newspaper ads for that matter) are considered "active candidates". These are people who are actively searching for jobs. They are clearly looking to make a move, as they are not satisfied with their current situation. Furthermore, they may or may not be currently employed. Searching a resume database allows the employer to attract a passive candidate. Most likely this candidate is currently employed. He or she might be quite happy in their current position but are willing to hear about potential opportunities.

The higher performers will typically fall under the passive candidate category. However, it is important to note that "A" players can and do apply for jobs. This is especially true in today's market where there are many talented people out of work. Just as you would create a high impact classified ad for a local newspaper, you want to take the same care in crafting your job posting. In fact, the posting allows you much more latitude than a newspaper ad because there is not a finite amount of space. Take advantage of this!

Give the job seekers enough information to educate themselves about the position and the company. Include details about the responsibilities of the position as well as the professional and personal characteristics you are looking for. By being clear about your requirements, you can minimize the number of unqualified applicants. Think about the individual you are targeting when crafting and posting your job. If you were looking for a Director of Food & Beverage for your hotel, would someone coming from the restaurant industry be a fit? If so, how likely is it for a restaurant executive searching jobs to come across a position in the lodging industry? Ask questions to your job board provider about how their search tools work. Job seekers are typically searching fields from a database so you want to ensure your jobs are visible to all candidates who may be a match. Searching resume databases is more time consuming than posting a job but it does significantly increase your chances of finding the high performer. Again, ask your job board operator for tips on how to best search their database.

A good approach is to first cast a wide net and then begin to narrow your criteria. Take a look at the list of job titles and note those positions that may be relevant. If you are looking for a Director of Sales, don't just search for people with that title. Would an Assistant Director of Sales at a larger property be qualified? Or even a Senior Sales Manager? Titles tend to get skewed between companies and cultures but skill sets remain the same. For example, an Assistant General Manager, Hotel Manager, Resident Manager, Executive Assistant Manager, Dir. Of Operations all may be the number two at their respective hotel properties. Don't miss out on talent by performing too narrow a search. This applies to keyword searches as well.

Company size and staffing needs dictate the amount of activity on a recruitment site. The usage may be as little as one job posting every couple of months to having human resource personnel searching databases day and night. Whatever your level of involvement, strive to be as efficient as possible in your internet recruiting and you will reap substantial rewards.

Online Service

Online sales have changed the face of hotel distribution. While 46% of U.S. hotel sales will be sold through the hotel call center in 2004, that figure will decline to 36% by 2006. At the same time, online sales will grow to nearly one-third of all hotel sales, according to From Property to Screen: Managing Online Hotel & Lodging Distribution, a new report by PhoCusWright Inc. Sales for both online travel agencies, such as Expedia and Travelocity, and hotel-branded Web sites will continue to grow, with the two channels battling for market share.

While hotels are enjoying increased control over their properties, as well as higher occupancy rates, third-party sites offer compelling sales and shopping options, and will continue to represent the greater share of Web hotel bookings. The report projects that online travel agencies will represent 54% of the market in 2006.

In 2003, the leading hotel chains stepped up their efforts to route business through their branded Web sites by improving functionality and offering Best Rate Guarantee programs that challenge customers to find lower rates on online travel sites. To lure customers, these sites also offer benefits for loyalty members, upgrades, looser cancellation policies, concierge services or other special features. Although hotels have struggled with price parity and rate integrity on the Web, they are finding that opaque sites, such as Priceline and Hotwire, are attractive vehicles for selling distressed inventory.

The online travel agency market shifted dramatically in the past year. There are several reasons why online travel agencies are experiencing such rampant growth:

— Accelerated merchant programs by Orbitz and Travelocity that increased sales for both sites.

— A dramatic increase in the percentage of total sales that come from hotels, as online travel agencies continue to promote the higher-margin product.

— An exploding international segment that already ranks Expedia among the top three online travel agencies in Europe. Although European online hotel sales are small compared to the U.S., they are growing rapidly and will significantly impact 2005-2006 growth rates.

— An increasing online presence for independent properties, which are being forced to invest in online travel agency distribution to compete with the chains and their brand prominence.

Several factors, including the improving economy and the increasing involvement of chains to provide properties with strategic advice, information systems, portals and negotiation power, are shifting the authority to control price, availability and content to local property management. However, the biggest obstacle to empowering managers at the local level is the absence of a fully integrated system and set of display screens with which to view the information needed to make critical channel distribution decisions.

— *From Property to Screen* is based on interviews with more than 50 executives from major U.S.-based hotel chains, Global Distribution Systems (GDSs), Distribution Service Providers (DSPs), Property Management Systems (PMSs), online travel agencies, technology companies, and other travel organizations. In addition, PhoCusWright conducted consumer research among online travelers in the U.S. and analyzed the online and offline service offerings of key distribution providers.

— *From Property to Screen:* Managing Online Hotel & Lodging Distribution is over 70 pages, including 40 tables and charts. Individual chapters examine the size of the market, hotel chain distribution strategies, the growth of online travel agencies and local property management's increasing role in channel and distribution decisions.

Suppliers and Online Travel Agencies

Market Size and Forecasts 2004-2006 estimates that while total travel industry growth rates will increase slightly each year, the online share of that market will continue to rise.

The result of this continuing shift of travel bookings to the Internet is that PhoCusWright projects more than one-third of all U.S. travel to be booked online by leisure and unmanaged business travel sites in 2006, up from 15% in 2002 and 20% in 2003. Many segments of the industry are walking a tightrope, with suppliers continuing to seek greater control over their inventory by drawing sales to their Web sites without alienating the online travel agencies that, in many cases, introduced them to Internet marketing. Within segments, there are varied differences. For example, independent hotel companies and cruise lines rely heavily on third party sites, while airlines, railways and car rental companies have strong online direct distribution.

In 2003, an even split marked the balance between online travel agency bookings and those completed on the supplier sites of airlines, hotels, car rental companies, traditional vacation packagers and cruise lines. This balance has been achieved following faster growth in supplier bookings in 2003, and is expected to remain constant as growth rates for both channels settle to comparable levels through 2006. Despite strong growth rates, there are barriers to online penetration that companies are aiming to eliminate.

Limitations to online sales in certain markets include the customer service requirements of cruise bookings, which entail many add-ons and options, and multi-leg air reservations. Just as the major online agencies helped to overcome earlier technological hurdles, suppliers have been upgrading their online customer service capabilities in an effort to bring the more complicated transactions, such as refunds/reissues/cancellations, online.

Protection from Injuries

The province's natural beauty is not the only reason tourists visit British Columbia. Many are attracted by its hotels and restaurants. Tourists, travellers, and residents alike visit hotels and restaurants for rest, leisure, convenience, and recreation. They rely on them for safety and comfort on vacations and business trips. The hotel and restaurant industries are an integral part of the province's economy. From 1986 to 1996, employment in hotels and restaurants grew over one-third, from 100,000 people in 1986 to 137,000 in 1996. The number of people employed in these industries in 1996 was approximately 7.6 percent of the work force. This is predicted to reach as high as 9.6 percent of the total B.C. work force by the year 2005.

The value of the goods and services produced by the hotel and restaurant industries — their gross domestic product (GDP) - also increased from 1986 to 1996. These industries contributed $2.2 billion to the B.C. economy in 1996. Furthermore, the demand for hotel rooms leads to the construction of new hotels, generating work for the construction industry. Growth in tourism, in turn, increases the demand for transportation and communications.

The hotel and restaurant industries employ a large number of young workers. This probably reflects the seasonal and part-time nature of staffing needs in these industries. They require more employees during the summer and weekends - times when young people are typically available to work. Workers of all ages are at risk of being seriously injured on the job in the hotel and restaurant industries, but the large number of young people employed in them highlights the importance of understanding the special concerns with working youth.

Though patrons associate them with comfort and enjoyment, hotels and restaurants are worksites, with real hazards and accidents. In 1996, hotels and restaurants accounted for about 6.3 percent of all time-loss claims accepted by the WCB. A time-loss claim is a claim for time lost due to an injury that results in a short-term disability, a long-term disability, or a fatality. From 1992 to 1996:

— 24,696 time-loss claims were accepted

— 616,674 days were lost from work due to workplace accidents

— 10 claims were accepted for fatalities Injury rates in the hotel and restaurant industries declined from four short-term disability claims per 100 person-years of employment in 1992, to three in 1996 - a drop of 25 percent. (Short-term disability claims are claims where a payment has been made for lost income.)

Since most of these injuries are preventable, injury rates are still higher than could be achieved. The WCB is working with employers and workers to continue this decline. Following are the costs the WCB paid out for claims in the hotel and restaurant industries from 1992 to 1996:

— Health-care benefits - $15.2 million.

— Rehabilitation costs - $2.6 million.

— Other costs - about $41 million. (These include wage loss and miscellaneous costs such as replacement glasses.)

The total costs the WCB paid out for claims in this five-year period were $58.8 million. The costs listed previously do not include other costs of workplace accidents and disease borne by employers, such as the costs of hiring replacement workers, overtime, and retraining. The pain, suffering, and disability experienced by workers as a result of workplace accidents are of even greater importance than the financial costs.

Hotel and restaurant workers occasionally find used needles and other items at work that could be contaminated with blood and body fluids infected with the viruses that cause HIV/AIDS, and hepatitis B and C. These items have been found between bedsheets, under beds, in garbage containers, and hidden in washrooms.

From 1992 to 1996 there were four reported needlestick injuries in the hotel industry and four in the restaurant industry. It's possible to become infected with a single exposure incident to infected blood and certain body fluids. The health effects of HIV/ AIDS and hepatitis B and C are serious.

Types of Accidents

Here are the four most common types of accidents that resulted in time-loss claims in the hotel industry from 1992 to 1996:

1. Overexertion - 27 percent of time-loss claims. These are injuries resulting from the application of force to an object or person - such as lifting, pushing, pulling, and carrying.
2. Being struck by an object - 16 percent. With this type of accident, the worker is injured by a moving object such as equipment and tools.
3. Falls on the same level - 14 percent (for example, slips).
4. Falls from elevations - 10 percent.

Overexertion accidents accounted for 27 percent of all claims accepted from 1992 to 1996. The following is a breakdown of overexertion accidents by the type of object handled:

— Handling containers accounted for 41 percent. Boxes, cartons, garbage cans or bags, trays, luggage or baggage, and buckets are examples of common containers.

— Moving fixtures and furniture (for example, beds, mattresses, tables, and sofas) contributed to 28 percent of these accidents.

— Handling laundry was responsible for 8 percent.

— Handling carts or grocery buggies contributed to 5 percent.

The occupations with the most overexertion accidents were:

— Room attendants - 39 percent

— Wait staff - 10 percent

— Kitchen helpers and laundry workers- 9 percent

— Chefs and cooks - 8 percent

Struck-by accidents

Being struck by an object or equipment caused 16 percent of all time-loss claims from 1992 to 1996 in the hotel industry. The types of equipment most often involved in these accidents were:

— Knives - 33 percent

— Food containers (for example, dishes, bowls, bottles, jars) - 14 percent

— Furniture (for example, tables, chairs, beds) - 8 percent

The occupations with the most struck-by accidents were:

— Chefs and cooks - 28 percent

— Room attendants - 17 percent

— Kitchen helpers and laundry workers- 16 percent

— Wait staff - 10 percent

Falls on the same level

Falls on the same level contributed to14 percent of all time-loss claims from 1992 to 1996. More than half were due to slippery surfaces, and 12 percent resulted from tripping or rough surfaces. Women had claims for falls on the same level two and a half times more often than men. The occupations with the most falls on the same level were:

— Room attendants - 33 percent

— Wait staff - 16 percent

— Chefs and cooks - 14 percent

— Kitchen and laundry workers- 12 percent

Falls from elevation

Ten percent of all time-loss claims from 1992 to 1996 in the hotel industry were falls from elevation. Of these falls:

— 38 percent were on or from stairs

— 11 percent were from objects not designed for standing on (for example, chairs)

— 6 percent were from ladders

The occupations with the most falls from elevation were:

— Room attendants - 24 percent

— Sports and recreation workers

— 17 percent

— Wait staff - 8 percent

Acts of violence and force

Workplace violence has become a growing concern for the hotel industry. From 1992 to 1996, three percent, or 250 claims, resulted from acts of violence or force in the workplace. Of these 250 claims:

— 70 percent were assaults without a weapon

— 24 percent were assaults with a weapon (for example, gun, knife)

— 6 percent were acts of force (that is, an act where it is not clear that there was an intent to injure - for example, a waiter who is injured while trying to break up a fight between customers)

The occupations with the most workplace violence accidents were:

— Bouncers, door attendants - 34 percent

— Bartenders - 16 percent

— Wait staff - 13 percent

— Desk clerks, reservation clerks - 8 percent

There are the four most common types of accidents in the restaurant industry from 1992 to 1996:

1. Being struck by an object - 24 percent. These are accidents where the worker is injured by a moving object such as equipment and tools.

2. Falls on the same level - 18 percent.

3. Burns and scalds - 16 percent.

4. Overexertion - 14 percent.

These are injuries resulting from the application of force to an object or person - such as lifting, pushing, pulling, and carrying.

Struck-by accidents

Being struck by an object or equipment caused 24 percent of the restaurant industry's accepted time-loss claims from 1992 to 1996. Accidents with a knife accounted for more than 60 percent of these struck-by accidents. The occupations with the most struck-by accidents were:

— Chefs and cooks - 46 percent

— Kitchen helpers or bus persons

— 33 percent

Falls on the same level

Falls on the same level accounted for 18 percent of all time-loss claims from 1992 to 1996. Seventy percent were caused by slippery surfaces, and 5 percent were due to tripping or rough surfaces. Women had claims for falls on the same level two and a half times more often than men. The occupations with the most falls on the same level were:

— Kitchen helpers or bus persons-35 percent

— Wait staff - 27 percent

— Chefs and cooks - 22 percent

Burns and scalds

Sixteen percent of all accidents in restaurants from 1992 to

1996 were burns and scalds. Contact with food products (for example, soup, tea, sauces) accounted for 39 percent of these burns and scalds, and 35 percent were the result of contact with fat, grease, or oil. The occupations with the most burns were:

— Chefs and cooks - 43 percent

— Kitchen helpers or bus persons - 32 percent

— Wait staff - 13 percent

Chemical burns are included in statistics on toxic exposures.

Overexertion

Overexertion contributed to 14 percent of all time-loss claims in the restaurant industry from 1992 to 1996. Of these, 82 percent were due to manual handling of containers, such as boxes and cartons. The occupations with the most overexertion accidents were:

— Chefs and cooks - 32 percent

— Kitchen helpers or bus persons - 31 percent

— Wait staff - 15 percent

Acts of violence and force

One percent - or 165 - of all claims in the restaurant industry resulted from acts of violence or force. Of these:

— 53 percent were assaults without a weapon.

— 43 percent were assaults with a weapon (for example, gun, knife)

— 4 percent were acts of force (that is, an act where it is not clear that there was an intent to injure - for example, a waiter who is injured while trying to break up a fight between customers)

The occupations with the most workplace violence accidents were:

— Bus persons - 26 percent

— Supervisors - 23 percent

In the fast-paced environment of hotels and restaurants, a common attitude is that accidents are inevitable and a part of doing business. But injuries mean losses. Lost money, lost time, and lost productivity. And more importantly, they mean that workers and their families suffer pain and have their lives disrupted. If accidents are prevented, the savings can be significant - less overtime, less retraining, and less time spent investigating accidents, to name a few. The other benefits are also rewarding - morale improves and workers feel valued.

Hotels and restaurants take pride in the service they offer tourists and other customers. Sometimes employees take customer satisfaction so seriously, they think of their customers ' safety before their own. Hotels and restaurants could prevent many workplace injuries by paying the same kind of attention to employee health and safety as they do to customer satisfaction.

Safety tips for preventing common accidents

This section contains lists of safety tips for preventing accidents that commonly occur in the hotel and restaurant industries. Safety tips are included on:

— Cuts

— Knives

— Slips and falls
— Floors
— Stairways
— Storage areas
— Burns and scalds
— Ladders

Cuts

Cuts can occur from:

— Knives
— Furniture
— Equipment
— Counters
— Utensils
— Glassware
— Preparation areas
— Dishes
— Cleaning equipment

Do

— Throw away broken or chipped glassware.
— Use a cutting board for safe cutting and chopping.
— Lock out or disconnect the power source before cleaning equipment such as meat slicers.
— Make sure that you receive proper training in operating equipment and safe job procedures.

— Consult the manufacturer's instruction manual for operating, cleaning, and maintaining the equipment.

— Make sure that cutting blades are sharp.

— After cleaning, make sure that all guards and safety devices are put back in place.

— Place a warning tag on defective and unsafe equipment and do not re-start the equipment. Inform your supervisor.

Do not

— Do not operate equipment if you feel unwell or drowsy. (Remember, some cold remedies can make people feel sleepy.)

— Do not place hands near the edge of cutting blades. Make sure you can always see both hands (and all fingers) and the cutting blades.

— Do not try to catch falling objects.

— Do not try to clean or "just brush something off" a moving part such as cutting blades or beaters in mixers.

— Do not push or place your hand in feed hoppers or delivery chutes. Use food pushers.

— Do not try to cut anything in a slicer that becomes too thin. Use a knife to finish cutting.

— Do not wear loose or frayed clothing, gloves, or jewellery that can be caught in a moving machine.

Knives

Potential injuries: cuts and amputation.

Do

- Use the right knife for the job.
- Always use a proper chopping board or block.
- Make sure the knife is sharp.
- Carry only one knife at a time, tip pointed down at your side.
- Store knives securely in proper racks in a visible place.
- Hold the knife with your stronger hand.
- Cut away from your body when cutting, trimming, or boning.
- When not using knives, place them at the back, with the sharp edge away from you.
- After using a knife, clean it immediately or place it in a dishwasher.
- Use protective clothing such as mesh gloves.

Do not

- Do not leave a knife in dishwater.
- Do not use a knife as a can opener.
- Do not try to catch a falling knife. Let it fall and then pick it up.
- Do not engage in horseplay with a knife in your hand.
- Do not carry knives while carrying other objects.
- Do not carry a knife in your pocket.
- Do not leave knives where they could be accidentally covered.
- Do not talk to your co-workers while you are using a knife - you could become distracted.

Slips and falls

Slips and falls can occur from:

— Slippery and cluttered floors and stairs

— Loose or bumpy carpets and floor mats

— Defective ladders and footstools

— Poor visibility

Do

— Keep floors and stairs clean, dry, and non-slippery.

— Keep floors and stairs clear of debris and obstruction.

— Use slip-resistant waxes to polish and treat floors.

— Make sure that carpeting, rugs, and mats are free of holes, loose threads, loose edges, and bumps that may cause tripping.

— Use adequate warning signs for wet floors and other hazards.

— Make sure that wooden duckboards and railings are in good repair and free of splinters.

— Make sure that ladders and footstools are in good repair and have non-skid feet.

— If possible, immediately remove or clean up any tripping or slipping hazard you notice. If it's not possible to take care of the hazard yourself, report it immediately to your supervisor.

Do not

— Do not use defective ladders or footstools.

— Do not use chairs, stools, or boxes as substitutes for ladders.

— Do not leave oven, dishwasher, or cupboard doors open. These may present a tripping hazard for you or your co-workers.

Floors

Potential accidents: slips and falls.

Do

— Make sure that walking surfaces are uncluttered, non-slippery, clean, and adequately lighted.

— If you drop or spill something, clean it up immediately.

— Mop floors with the recommended amount of cleaning product in the water, or cleaning fluid, to ensure grease and other slippery substances are removed.

— Make sure floors are free from trip hazards such as raised or broken sections.

— Treat floors with slip-resistant products if the floors must be waxed.

— Place wet floor warning signs to prevent people from slipping.

— Use non-slip mats and floor finishes.

— Replace doormats regularly.

— Walk - don't run.

— Mark swinging doors with in and out signs.

Do not

— Do not leave carts, boxes, trash cans, or other objects on the floors and in the aisles.

Stairways

Potential accidents: slips and falls.

Do

—Ensure that stairways are well lit.

— Keep stairs clear of obstructions.

— Use handrails.

— When carrying a load up and down stairs, make sure that the load does not block your vision.

— Report tripping hazards to your supervisor and place warning signs.

Do not

— Do not store boxes and supplies on the stairs.

— Do not throw things up or down stairways.

— Do not switch off lights in the stairways.

Storage Areas

Potential hazards: collapse of stored goods; slipping and tripping.

Do

— Make sure the shelves are firmly secured in place against walls and on the floor.

— Ensure adequate lighting.

— Store chemicals, detergents, and pesticides in a separate area away from foodstuff.

— Ensure that chemicals that are not compatible with each other are not stored together.

— Store heavy items on lower shelves, particularly when cartons contain fluids.

— Use bins and racks as much as possible.

— Leave adequate clearance space between the top of the stored goods and the ceiling in areas protected by a sprinkler system.

— Store cartons in dry areas.

Do not

— Do not block passages in the storage area.

— Do not stack loose items on the top shelves.

— Do not overload shelving units.

— Do not store cardboard cartons in damp areas.

— Do not overstock.

Ladders

Potential accidents: falls from portable ladders; splinters; slipping.

Do

— Inspect a ladder before and after each use.

— Reject a ladder if it has loose, broken, or missing rungs; loose hinges; or loose or missing screws or bolts.

— Reject and tag defective ladders. Have defective ladders repaired or thrown out.

— Use a ladder designed for your task.

Consider strength, type, and Canadian Standards Association (CSA) or American National Standards Institute (ANSI) approval.

— Set up barricades and warning signs when using a ladder in a doorway or passageway.

— Clean muddy or slippery footwear before mounting a ladder.

— Face the ladder when going up or down and when working from it.

— Keep the centre of your body within the side rails.

— Place ladder feet 30 cm (1 ft.) from the wall for every 1 m (3 ft.) of height.

— Extend the ladder at least 1 m (3 ft.) above the landing platform.

— Locate the ladder on a firm footing using slip-resistant feet or secure blocking, or have someone hold the ladder.

— Rest both side rails on a top support, and secure the ladder to prevent slipping.

— Use a three-point stance, keeping both feet and at least one hand on the ladder at all times.

Do not

— Do not use ladder in a horizontal position as a scaffold plank or runway.

— Do not carry objects in your hands while on a ladder. Hoist materials or attach tools to a belt.

— Do not work from the top two rungs. The higher you go on a ladder, the greater the possibility that the ladder will slip out at the base.

— Do not use makeshift items such as a chair, barrel, milk crate, or box as a substitute for a ladder.

Burns and scalds

Burns and scalds can occur from:

— Stoves o Toasters

— Toaster ovens o Ovens

— Boiling hot liquid o Hot utensils

— Pressure cookers o Cooking pots

— Hot dishwashers

Do

— Assume that all pots and pans and metal handles are hot. Touch them only when you are sure that they are not hot or when you are using proper gloves.

— Organize your work area to prevent contact with hot objects and flames.

— Keep pot handles away from hot burners.

— Make sure that handles of pots and pans do not stick out from the counter or cooking stove.

— Use oven mitts appropriate for handling hot objects. Use long gloves for deep ovens.

— Follow electric and fire safety guidelines.

— Follow the manufacturer's operating instructions.

— Use only recommended temperature settings for each type of cooking.

— Open hot water and hot liquid faucets slowly to avoid splashes.

— Lift lids by opening away from you.

— Wear long-sleeved cotton shirts and cotton pants.

— Report problems to your supervisor.

Do not

- Do not overfill pots and pans.
- Do not leave metal spoons in pots and pans while cooking.
- Do not spill water in hot oil.
- Do not overstretch over a stove, grill, or other hot area in order to reach an uncomfortable distance.
- Do not use a wet cloth to lift lids from hot pots.
- Do not open cookers and steam ovens that are under pressure.
- Do not lean over pots of boiling liquids.
- Do not leave a hot electric element or gas flame of stove "on" all the time.

Young worker focus

Workers of all ages face hazards on the job. However, a number of factors raise special concerns about working youth.

- The rates of work-related injury to males aged 15 to 24 have historically been higher than the rates of injuries to males aged 25 and over and much higher than among females of all ages.
- In 1997, 10 out of 95 (11 percent) of traumatic work-related fatalities reported to the WCB involved workers aged 24 or younger.
- Workers aged 15 to 24 sustained approximately 16 percent of all disability claims in 1996 and they constituted 14.5 percent of the work force. (About 70 percent of those aged 15 to 19 and 24 percent of those

aged 20 to 24 work only part-time, so the occurrence of injuries and fatalities could be expected to be somewhat lower than average in this age group.)

— Young workers typically work at a series of part-time, temporary, minimum-wage jobs, often going to their jobs after putting in the equivalent of a day of work at school.

— As new workers, young people are likely to be inexperienced and unfamiliar with many of the tasks required of them, unable to recognize workplace hazards, and unaware of their rights as workers. Many positive youthful traits such as energy, enthusiasm, and a need for increased challenges and responsibility, combined with a reluctance to ask questions or make demands of their employers, can result in young workers taking on tasks for which they are neither prepared nor capable of doing safely.

— Youth have an awareness that if they cause trouble at work there is always a surplus of workers to replace them. This contributes to young people's reticence refuse jobs and activities that might place them in danger.

— The level of physical development of young workers is also important to consider. Adolescents, especially males, between the ages of 15 and 19, experience growth spurts at very different rates, which have consequences for either extreme. Smaller workers may not be able to reach parts of machines and may lack the strength required for certain tasks designed to be carried out by adults. Larger youths may be given adult tasks simply because of their size without regard to their lack of experience and maturity.

— Young workers are often employed in retail industries. Settings in which the exchange of money occurs are thought be at an increased risk for workplace violence. Other risk factors that increase the dangers for youth working in these settings include working alone and working late in the evening and early morning - hours that fit many young people's schedules.

— Several U.S. reports suggest that young people generally do not receive adequate prevention training either in school or on the job. As they have little experience in the work force in generaı, they also do not recognize how much training may be necessary. Furthermore, many of the training materials that are available are not geared to youth.

As the workplace is made safer in general, it will be safer for young workers. At the same time, young workers deserve special attention and certain prevention efforts should be targeted specifically at young workers. These include:

— Eliminating hazards through redesign of the workplace or work processes in jobs commonly held by youth.

— Early orientation and instruction, preferably from the moment the young worker steps onto the worksite.

— Educating young workers, parents, employers, health providers, and school personnel about health and safety hazards and about workplace rights and responsibilities.

— Expanding the base of information about occupational injuries to guide prevention activities, including efforts to encourage the reporting of all incidents and injuries occurring to young people at work. This includes the reporting of even those accidents and injuries that do not lead to lost time.

— Emphasizing to employers the importance of tailoring workplace policies to young workers. For example, there may be times when a "customer is always right" policy may be necessary in order to reduce the threat of violence.

— Extra observation of young workers by all supervisors and co-workers to protect the safety and well-being of new workers.

Employers and supervisors can make work safer for young workers

— Know and comply with safety requirements that apply to your workplace. Post these requirements where workers can see and read them. Assess and eliminate the potential for injury and illness associated with tasks required of young workers.

— Provide comprehensive training to ensure young workers recognize hazards and are competent in safe work practices.

— Routinely check that young workers continue to recognize hazards and use safe work practices.

— Evaluate equipment that young workers might be required to operate to ensure that it is safe for their use.

— Ensure that young workers are appropriately supervised to prevent injuries and hazardous exposures.

— Involve supervisors and experienced workers in developing a workplace health and safety program and in identifying and solving potential health and safety problems.

Young workers can do

- Be aware that you have the right to work in a safe and healthy work environment free of recognized hazards and that you have the right to refuse unsafe work tasks and conditions.
- Know that you have the right to file complaints with the WCB when you feel your health and safety rights have been violated or your safety has been compromised.
- Remember that all workers, including young and part-time workers, are entitled to workers' compensation benefits in the event of a work-related injury or illness.
- Obtain information about your rights and responsibilities as workers from school counsellors or the WCB.
- Participate in all training programs offered by your employer, or request training if none is offered.
- Recognize and be aware of the potential for injury at work and seek information about safe work procedures from employers.
- Identify the first aid attendant at your workplace.
- Locate the first aid kit at your workplace.
- Always use safety equipment and follow safe work practices.

Preventing overexertion accidents

Risk factors

The key to preventing injuries is to reduce or eliminate the risk factors contributing to the injuries. Workplace factors associated with overexertion accidents to the back include:

— Awkward back posture held for a period of time or repeated due to poor or king heights and reaches. Examples include reaching for linen or supplies located on high shelves.

— Heavy or frequent lifting, pushing, pulling, and carrying. For example, lifting and carrying bulk food containers.

— Prolonged sitting or standing. Examples include:

— Sitting - front office staff working on computers

— Standing - a restaurant worker whose duties consist of greeting customers and working the cash

— Whole body vibration. For example, delivery truck drivers.

How to reduce overexertion accidents

Reducing risks need not be a complicated process. Following are examples of solutions in the hotel and restaurant industries:

— Store heavier or frequently used items at a height between workers' hips and chest to reduce awkward postures when handling these items.

— Place smaller loads in laundry washing machines to reduce tangling and the subsequent heavy pulling needed to remove the laundry from the washer.

— Use laundry carts with spring-loaded bottoms that rise as the cart is unloaded. This reduces repetitive, awkward bending.

— Install platforms at the base of laundry chutes to eliminate repetitive bending and lifting from the floor while sorting laundry.

— Use long-handled tools to reach the walls and tub when cleaning showers to decrease reaching and stooping.

— Ask a co-worker for help when moving heavy furniture. Employers should set a policy to give guidance in these situations.

— Ensure cleaning products and equipment are efficient and do not require extra force to use. For example, use a window cleaner that doesn't streak to reduce the number of wiping motions, or use a cleanser that removes dirt and grime with one swipe.

— Use smaller banquet trays to lighten loads and to make them easier to handle.

— Store clean plates on spring-loaded dollies to reduce repetitive bending.

— Use carts to move heavy products from storage coolers and freezers.

— Don't store heavy items in small, confined areas where the worker may not be able to use safe lifting techniques.

— Design or alter "pass through" windows in restaurants to reduce the risk of back injury. If they are too high or too deep, workers are forced to use long reaches and awkward postures to pick up orders.

— Lower storage racks at dishwasher stations to minimize awkward lifting and reaching. Lowering the racks or using a sturdy step stool can help to reduce the height of the lift.

— Add a footrest or matting to a hostess counter to give some relief from prolonged standing.

— Reduce risks through organizing work differently. For example, room attendants could unload laundry from their carts more often to lighten the loads they handle and to reduce the amount of pushing needed to move the cart.

— Train and supervise workers in safe workpractices that have been developed to reduce their exposure to risk factors.

Preventing exposure to HIV/AIDS, and hepatitis B and C at work

Hotel and restaurant workers sometimes find used needles between bedsheets, under beds, in garbage containers, and hidden in washrooms. Sometimes cleaning staff come into contact with condoms when they try to unclog toilets. These items could be contaminated with blood and body fluids infected with tiny organisms that can cause disease in humans. These micro-organisms are known as bloodborne pathogens. The bloodborne pathogens of most concern are the human immunodeficiency virus (HIV) and the hepatitis B and C viruses.

HIV causes the disease AIDS (acquired immune deficiency syndrome), and the hepatitis B and hepatitis C viruses cause diseases with the same names. Since exposure to blood and certain body fluids may spread these viruses, these diseases are also called bloodborne diseases.

Most hotel and restaurant workers won't ever contact, at work, blood and certain body fluids that can spread HIV and the hepatitis B and C viruses. But even employers and workers in settings where contact with blood and these body fluids is not expected should be aware of some basic precautions because it is possible to become infected with a single exposure incident - that is, harmful contact to infected blood and body fluids. This section provides information on the basic precautions that should be taken in such work settings.

Hepatitis B and C should not be confused with hepatitis A - a foodborne illness. That means that you can become infected with the hepatitis A virus if you eat food that has been prepared by someone who is infected with the virus. Hepatitis A is primarily a public health concern. Hotel and restaurant owners who would like more information on how to prevent the spread of hepatitis A should contact their local health units.

Workers can be exposed to infected blood and body fluids at work in the following ways:

- By puncturing the skin with sharp objects contaminated with infected blood and body fluids. (Sharp objects are commonly known as sharps. These include needles, scalpels, knives, razors, scissors, broken glass, or anything that can pierce, puncture, or cut skin.)
- By splashing infected blood and body fluids into the tissues lining the eyes, nose, or mouth. These tissues are called mucous membranes.
- By splashing infected blood and body fluids on non-intact skin - that is,fresh open cuts, nicks, wounds, skin abrasions, chapped and damaged skin, and skin with diseases such as eczema and dermatitis.

Reduce the risk of infection at work

Where it is reasonable to expect that workers could be exposed to blood and certain body fluids as part of their normal job duties, employers must comply with the sections on biohazardous materials in Part 6 of the Occupational Health and Safety Regulation. Under these requirements, employers will typically have to develop and implement exposure control plans that eliminate or minimize the specific risks and hazards in their workplaces.

Accident investigations are an important source of health and safety information. If a review of accident reports shows that exposure incidents involving blood and certain body fluids have occurred in the past, an exposure control plan may be required. There's a lot of concern in the workplace about HIV/AIDS, and hepatitis B and C. Even if contact is not likely to occur at a worksite, the employer can help allay such concern and can ensure that workers are prepared for unexpected events. To do this, employers should:

— Inform and instruct workers in how to eliminate or reduce the risk of contact with blood and certain body fluids

— Ensure that work practices eliminate or minimize the risk of unforeseen contact Develop ways to address chance encounters with blood and certain body fluids

— Provide workers with the equipment, tools, and personal protective equipment (PPE) needed to deal with an unforeseen contact

— Monitor the workplace to ensure that safeguards are used and safe work practices are followed

— In case of an exposure incident, ensure that:

— Prompt, easy-to-access first aid and medical attention is available

— Employees are aware of procedures for obtaining immediate first aid and medical attention and for reporting incidents of exposure to blood and certain body fluids

If an exposure incident occurs at the workplace, the employer must investigate it and, based on the findings, must develop ways to prevent similar incidents from occurring.

Safe work practices

Safe work practices explain how tasks are to be performed to reduce the likelihood of exposure to hazards. Even if workers aren't expected to be in contact with blood and certain body fluids, all workplaces should have basic safe work practices to deal with the rare incidents that could occur. The sample safe work practices in this section can be used to guide you in developing similar ones tailored to your workplace. Specific information about your workplace should be added, where relevant, or where it is needed to clarify instructions. Examples of the types of information that should be added include:

— Specific instructions on how to summon first aid and seek medical attention

— The person to report exposure incidents to

— What PPE (such as waterproof gloves) is required, when to use it, and how to obtain it

— The location of equipment and tools such as sharps containers, tongs, and spill kits

Don't pick up sharps and other items (for example, condoms) unless you have the appropriate equipment and PPE and you have been instructed how to do so safely. Don't pick up anything with the intention of discarding it later. For example, don't put a used needle in your pocket that isn't in a proper pocket container. You could injure yourself before you discard it. Do not place needles in regular garbage under any circumstances - you may create a hazard for others. Follow these steps to pick up improperly discarded sharps and other items that could carry HIV and the hepatitis B and C viruses:

1. Wear disposable waterproof gloves (such as natural rubber latex, neoprene, nitrile, and vinyl), and have a proper sharps container and tongs or pliers ready. (You can obtain sharps containers from safety and medical supply stores and some municipal needle exchange programs. Drug stores may also carry suitable containers.)

2. Put the gloves on. Place the sharps container next to the needle or other item. Don't hold the container in your hand, or you might accidentally jab yourself.

3. If you are comfortable using tongs or pliers, use them to pick up the needle (or other item) and place it into the sharps container. This is the preferred method. If you are not comfortable using the tongs or pliers, pick up the needle by its shaft - with your gloved hand. In both cases, place the needle into the sharps container, pointed end first, away from you. Do not insert fingers into the opening of the container, and keep the free hand out of the way.

4. Remove and discard the gloves . Wash your hands with soap and water.

5. Don't fill the sharps container to the brim. When it is about three-quarters full, replace it with a new one and properly dispose of the old one. Contact your municipality for information on disposal.

Remove disposable gloves as soon as possible if they become damaged or ontaminated. Remove them after you have completed the task that required gloves. Gloves should also be removed before leaving the work area. Do not wash and reuse your gloves. Use new gloves for each new task. Follow these steps to make sure your hands do not contact any blood or body fluids left on used gloves:

1. With both hands gloved:
   - Grasp the outside of one glove at the top of the wrist.
   - Peel off this glove from wrist to fingertips while turning it inside out, as you pull the glove off your hand and away from you.
   - Hold the glove you just removed in your gloved hand.
2. With the ungloved hand:
   - Peel off the second glove by inserting your fingers on the inside at the top of your wrist.
   - Turn the glove inside out while pulling it away from you, leaving the first glove inside the second.
3. Dispose of the entire bundle promptly in a suitable waterproof garbage bag.
4. Wash your hands thoroughly with soap and water as soon as possible after removing gloves and before touching noncontaminated objects and surfaces.

Follow these steps to prevent contact with sharps and other items improperly discarded in garbage:

1. Handle garbage as little as possible.
2. Use waterproof garbage bags.

3. Be alert. If possible, look for sharps sticking out of the bags. Listen for broken glass when you move the bag.
4. Don't compress garbage or reach into garbage containers with your bare hands.
5. Don't use your bare hands to pick up garbage that has spilled out of an overflowing container. Wear punctureresistant and liquid-resistant gloves (the type worn by firefighters), or use other tools designed for picking up garbage.
6. Don't let garbage bags get too full, if possible. Leave enough free space at the top of the bag, so that when you grab it, you grab the top of the bag only - not any of the contents. You may have to change bags more often to prevent them from getting too full. This will also make them lighter - and thus easier to hold away from your body.
7. Hold garbage bags by the top of the bag, away from your body. Don't hold garbage bags against your body.
8. Don't place one hand under the bag to support it.
9. Dispose of wastes according to federal, provincial, and local regulations.

The following exposure incidents are potentially harmful:

— Skin is punctured with a contaminatedsharp.

— A mucous membrane (the eyes, nose, or mouth) is splashed with blood and certain body fluids.

— Non-intact skin is splashed with blood and certain body fluids.

If any of the above incidents occurs, follow these steps:

1. Get first aid immediately. If the mucous membranes

of the eyes, nose, or mouth are affected, flush with lots of clean water at a sink or eyewash station.

— If there is a sharps injury, allow the wound to bleed freely. Then wash the area thoroughly with non-abrasive soap and water.

— If an area of non-intact skin is affected, wash the area thoroughly with non-abrasive soap and water.

2. Report the incident. Report the incident as soon as possible to your supervisor and first aid attendant, or occupational health staff. This should not cause significant delay in seeking medical attention.

3. Seek medical attention immediately. Seek medical attention immediately - preferably within two hours - at the closest hospital emergency room, or at a health care facility if there's no hospital emergency room in the vicinity. Immunizations or medications may be necessary. These may prevent infection or favourably alter the course of the disease if you do become infected. Blood tests should also be done at that time. You may need to see your family doctor within the next five days for follow-up, such as counselling and medications.

4. Complete WCB claim forms. If the exposure incident occurred at work, the employer and worker must complete and submit the appropriate WCB claim forms. For any questions about claims, contact the WCB Occupational Disease Service at 604 276-3007 or 1 800 661-2112. Blood and certain body fluid contact with intact skin is not considered to be a risk for the spread of bloodborne pathogens. You should, however, thoroughly wash your hands and other affected areas immediately. If you have any further

concerns, contact your family physician or nearest health unit office .

Once any exposure incident has been attended to, clean up spills as soon as possible. Don't clean up blood and certain body fluids unless you have been trained to do so and have the equipment needed to do so safely. Kits that contain the supplies needed to clean up spills are available from safety supply companies. Procedures for cleaning up spilled blood and certain body fluids should include the following steps:

1. Restrict access to the area.
2. Make sure plastic bags are available for removal of contaminated items from the spill site. Have bleach or a germicide ready.
3. Dispose of any sharps.
4. Wear disposable, waterproof gloves (such as natural rubber latex, neoprene, nitrile, and vinyl). If necessary, wear other PPE, such as a face shield and a gown, to act as a barrier against contact with blood and certain body fluids and the dilute household bleach.
5. Cover your shoes or boots with disposable, waterproof covers if they could become contaminated during clean-up.
6. Wipe up visible material first with disposable towels (or in another way that prevents direct contact with blood and body fluids). Dispose of the material and paper towels in waterproof garbage bags.
7. After you have carefully wiped up all the obvious material, it may be necessary to change gloves. Then decontaminate the area by carefully pouring over the spill site a germicide approved for used as a hospital disinfectant, or a fresh solution of household bleach

and water. Leave the solution on for 10 minutes, then wipe it up with disposable towels. Discard the towels in the waterproof garbage bags.

8. Clean and decontaminate all soiled, reusable equipment and supplies. Properly discard any disposable items.
9. Wear the gloves to remove other protective equipment such as face shields and footwear covers. Dispose of or clean PPE (for example, face shields, aprons, boot covers) according to the manufacturer's directions.
10. Properly remove and dispose of your gloves. Wash your hands.

Health and Safety Program

Everyone who works for a hotel or restaurant must work safely and encourage others to do the same. But it's the employer who must develop and implement policies and procedures to prevent workplace injury and diseases in a systematic way. Hotels and restaurants with 50 or more workers are required to establish formal health and safety programs; those with fewer than 50 employees are required to establish less formal programs. This section describes the elements that make up an effective health and safety program. It also reviews the elements of an effective subprogram, specifically a violence prevention program.

Health and safety programs must be written and the program documents must describe how the employer will manage health and safety. The written program must:

— Provide general direction to management, supervisors, and workers about their responsibilities and roles in providing a safe and healthy workplace. Provide specific direction to those responsible for a portion of the program.

— Communicate health and safety policies and procedures.
— Open the lines of communication by encouraging workers to express their concerns about health and safety.

An effective program needs the support of management, the participation of workers, an effective health and safety committee (where the workplace is large enough to require one), and regular program reviews. The WCB requires employers to set up programs tailored to the size and the specific needs of their companies. Each program element plays an important role in providing a safe, healthy workplace.

Proactive elements

The first six elements of the health and safety program are considered proactive elements because they all play a role in the recognition, assessment, elimination, and control of workplace hazards.

1. *Policy:*The policy states the program's goals and communicates management's commitment to health and safety. It states the responsibilities of the employer, managers, supervisors, and workers.

2. Written work procedures Written work procedures include the rules and safe work procedures developed to control hazards. They are management's directions detailing how the work is expected to be carried out safely.

3. Training of workers and supervisors. It's management's responsibility to ensure that everyone who performs a hazardous task is trained to follow the safe work procedures that have been developed. Workers and supervisors must receive training.

4. Management and supervision of workers The supervisor's first responsibility is to ensure that workers have been properly instructed and directed in the safe performance of their duties. Training (element 3) will satisfy this first responsibility. A supervisor's second responsibility is to ensure that trained workers follow the directions provided. Managers have responsibilities to ensure the health and safety program is properly directed and controlled. These include:

   — Monitoring implementation of the program

   — Discussing health and safety issues at staff and management meetings

   — Ensuring that health and safety is given adequate consideration in all management decisions

   — Developing a system of progressive discipline to be used if workers, supervisors, and managers deliberately ignore safety rules and regulatory requirements

5. *Regular inspections*: The identification of hazards - existing or potential - is an ongoing task because the workplace is a dynamic place. Changes occur for a variety of reasons. Some changes occur slowly (such as normal wear and tear on equipment and fixtures); other changes occur because a process is modified or something new is added. Tasks may be performed differently, creating hazards (such as unsafe acts). Regular inspections provide the means to continually

monitor the workplace for changing conditions and unsafe conditions and acts. The results of these inspections can lead to changes in written work procedures, training , and supervision .

6. *Hazardous materials and substances:* This element requires that all workers be able to recognize the harmful substances and materials they might encounter in their work areas. The Workplace Hazardous Materials Information System (WHMIS) is designed to provide employers with the necessary information about these hazardous products to ensure they are handled, used, and stored properly. Reactive elements: The next three elements can be described as reactive elements because they "respond" to injured workers, diseases, and accidents that occur.

7. *Medical examination and monitoring* :In some cases, the health of workers must be followed to determine if working conditions have caused or may cause an occupational disease. Examples include workers who may have had contact with an infectious organism (for example, hepatitis B and C viruses, and HIV) and workers who require annual hearing tests because they are exposed routinely to excessive noise.

8. *First aid:* The purpose of first aid is to provide workers with prompt, accessible, appropriate first aid treatment, and to keep records of each treatment.Effective first aid programs lower employers' staffing costs and WCB claims costs because minor injuries can be treated at the worksite. This element addresses how first aid will be administered in the workplace to comply with occupational first aid requirements.

9. *Investigation of incidents, accidents, and diseases:*It's an unfortunate circumstance when a worker gets hurt on the job. It's even worse if no attempt is made to learn and correct the causes that led to the accident and worker injury.If the causes are not corrected, more workers may be injured in a similar manner. This element addresses how investigations of incidents, accidents, and diseases are to be conducted in order to find the causes and prevent recurrence.

Administrative elements

A health and safety program must be properly administered to be effective. The final three elements outline the administrative requirements of the program.

10. *Health and safety committee:* In the hotel and restaurant industry, a health and safety committee is required at workplaces with 20 or more employees. The committee must have at least four regular members and the number of employer representatives must not outnumber worker representatives. In smaller workplaces (more than 9 but fewer than 20 regular employees), a worker health and safety representative is required.

The committee monitors health and safety and makes recommendations to management on improvements. The written program should describe how the committee is to be structured, its terms of reference, and its roles and duties.

11. *Records and statistics:* Records and statistics help identify trends, unusual conditions, and problem areas. They are compiled to provide a performance measurement of the health and safety program and for guidance to set goals throughout the organization.

Records and statistics can also be used for educational purposes. Examples of records and statistics that should be kept include:

- — Accident and incident reports
- — Hazard reports
- — Training records
- — First aid treatment book
- — Equipment log books
- — Maintenance records
- — Statistics on the frequency and severity of accidents

12. *Review of the health and safety program:* A systematic and critical examination of the entire workplace should be carried out at least annually. A review is intended to examine the extent and effectiveness of existing health and safety activities and to identify deficiencies.

Where a hazard is responsible for a significant portion of total injuries or diseases at the workplace, management must address that hazard in a systematic way. The best way to do this is to apply the elements of the health and safety program to the specific hazard and create a sub-program. Violence is a good example. From 1992 to 1996, violent incidents in the hotel and restaurant industry resulted in 4 fatalities, 162 accepted claims from restaurants, and 250 accepted claims from hotels. For this reason, hotels and restaurants must develop workplace violence prevention programs. These violence prevention programs should contain essentially the same elements as the general health and safety program such as a policy, written work procedures, training of supervisors and workers, accident investigations, records and statistics, and the commitment of the employer.

4

Service Management

Product-development and marketing managers know that customers make purchasing decisions on the basis of many criteria, including service quality, delivery speed and price. But since no company can excel in all aspects of service delivery simultaneously, companies must make trade-offs on the basis of what they do best, what criteria matter most to their customers, and what their competitors are offering.

An August 2002 white paper, 'Understanding Customer Value Drivers: A Key to Successful Service Management,' offers managers a way to assess customers' choices in order to optimize return on their product-development and customer-service investments. Authors Rohit Verma, associate professor of operations management at the University of Utah's Eccles School of Business, and Gerhard Plaschka, associate professor of management at DePaul University's Kellstadt Graduate School of Business, base their framework upon choice modeling (CM) — an approach first introduced in the 1970s by Daniel L. McFadden, Nobel Prize-winning professor of economics at the University of California, Berkeley.

McFadden's research focused on both the economic reasons for individual choices and the ways researchers could measure and predict these choices. He began with the macroeconomic theory that says people will act to maximize their self-interest and applied it to the most complex microeconomic choices, such as why people take certain jobs, whether they marry, and how they travel to work. McFadden's work subsequently led to applications in various fields, including marketing, natural resource economics and transportation, as well as service management.

Verma and Plaschka believe that most companies lack a clear understanding of their relevant customer and market drivers and, as a result, their product or marketing managers tend to take a scattershot approach, hoping that at least one product-service offering will succeed. Using McFadden's theories and subsequent work on experimental choice analysis (introduced by Jordan Louviere of the University of Technology, Sydney, and other researchers), the authors developed a three-step process to assess and challenge management preconceptions of how customer offerings will be received.

CM links theoretical behavior — observed in experiments, surveys and other forms of stated preferences — with behavior observed in real-life situations. Unlike conjoint analysis (in which study respondents rank their preferences using experimental profiles), CM requires that respondents make choices in simulated situations derived from realistic variations of expected market offerings. The process comprises three steps.

First, using qualitative market assessment, customer interviews, case studies, industry data, focus groups and other information sources, managers compile a list of market-value drivers that they believe influence customers' buying decisions. For example, a hotel manager might identify choice drivers and value levels such as 'hotel type' (motel, bed & breakfast inn, boutique hotel, convention hotel), 'loyalty program' (hotel points, merchant points, airline frequent-flier miles), 'amenities' (in-room business center, central business kiosk, anytime check-in/check-out), 'eating options' (full-service restaurant, breakfast-only restaurant, in-room kitchenette), and 'price' (weekday rate, weekend rate, all-inclusive pricing options). Participants must collectively finalize a list of drivers, limited enough not to overwhelm potential study respondents but realistic enough to reflect the actual market.

Next, managers construct 'choice' experiments, asking respondents to select a set of options from a bundle of product and service attributes. For example, a hotel operator might describe two possible hotels, listing a number of market drivers and specific value levels for each. Respondents then answer questions about the choices. Because the number of potential attribute configurations can multiply quickly — 10 drivers with four value levels each can generate more than a million alternatives — experiment designers can employ statistical techniques (such as fractional factorial design and blocking) to estimate the impact of major drivers; then they can divide these choice exercises into statistically equivalent subgroups.

In the final phase, econometric models (based on discrete choice analysis) are used to identify key patterns in the survey responses, providing relative weighting for each market value driver and for interactions among drivers. Managers can then select the optimal combination of operations and market drivers in order to develop a profitable and sustainable value proposition that, under normal competitive constraints, will maximally leverage their available resources.

Like other modeling processes, choice modeling is subject to the 'garbage in, garbage out' rule. It generates useful information only if the assumptions behind the selection of value drivers, the experiment design and the data-collection methods are sound. If these conditions are met, Verma and Plaschka suggest, CM can yield valuable insights for market-strategy development by revealing customer clusters, suggesting the potential impact of changing the levels of value drivers, assessing overall brand equity and identifying barriers to brand switching. Moreover, CM can reveal any salient differences between managers' beliefs about customers' needs and their actual needs.

In a number of projects, the authors have applied CM to several industries, including telecommunications, financial services, industrial services, outdoor recreation and banking, among others. CM analysis can help managers design attractive offerings and hone their company's operations. For example, if CM reveals that hotel customers value anytime check-in/check-out over a customer-loyalty program, managers could improve the back-end processes that support faster check-in/check-out service. For managers eager for reliable feedback on how consumers view their offerings, the authors say, CM provides a rigorous way to turn that feedback into profitable and sustainable strategies for retaining or capturing market share and profitability.

Electronic Distribution

The number of reservations flowing to hotels through the electronic distribution channels – the global distribution systems and the Internet – is growing steadily. Once a minor contributor of bookings, they are now primary business sources and grow more important with every passing month. This productivity growth has heightened emphasis throughout the hotel industry on using the electronic distribution channels effectively and maximizing their potential.

Every director of sales and marketing faces the challenge of understanding, prioritizing and managing these electronic outlets on behalf of his or her property. How important is electronic distribution as a means of gaining reservations? The Hotel Electronic Distribution Network Association (HEDNA) reported that in 1999 the global distribution systems delivered over 43 million bookings with a value in excess of $12.5 billion. GDS booking growth continues at about 10 percent a year. Everyone has his or her own stories of the impact of the Internet. Some large chains are experiencing 200-300 percent growth annually.

Some small, boutique properties report that over 75 percent of their bookings now come from the Web. Regardless of the Internet's current reservation production for your hotel, it bears only modest resemblance to the broader and ever-expanding impact it will have in the future. As the number of people who have Internet access approaches 100 million in the United States and 200 million worldwide, research repeatedly indicates that consumers are turning to the Internet for travel-related information. They may not book online (although they will eventually), but they are already comparing you with your competitors before they pick up their telephone to call your CRO or drive up to the front door of your property.

As a hotel sales and marketing professional your limited resources are allocated to presenting your property in the sales channels that will be the most productive for you—be they print ads, direct mail, public relations, sales calls or electronic distribution channel participation and advertising. You strive to select the most cost-effective and compelling channels, that will in turn bring guests to your door and put heads in your beds. This resource allocation process requires assessment of each potential business source's target audience, opportunities for participation, probable production and costs. This applies to electronic distribution just as it does to other sales options. Narrowing the focus to the electronic distribution channels, the two broadest categories are global distribution systems (GDS) and Internet web sites.

Global Distribution Systems (GDS)

The GDSs, of which there are four major competitors including Amadeus, Galileo/Apollo, Sabre and Worldspan, originated as private networks for use by travel agents. In the 35 years since their inception, they have grown to serve a worldwide clientele who use nearly 500,000 access points. They have expanded from listing only air flights to presenting the full array of travel services. Recently, they have moved to make their rich databases of travel service information available to web sites – both their own and others managed by third parties. Key considerations in evaluating GDS significance for your hotel include:

— Worldwide, 24/7 availability

— Extensive use by travel agents

— Most common booking mechanism for consortia and negotiated corporate rates

— Expanding their leisure product offerings

— Little maintenance effort required - information provided to the central reservation system for your hotel chain or representation company is copied automatically to all four of the GDSs

An individual hotel automatically participates in the GDS as part of their membership in a hotel chain or representation company. This base level involvement provides the display of available room types and the rates for those rooms, for any date(s) in the coming 12 months, and a display of an extensive description of the hotel. To improve its presentation in the GDSs, your hotel has several options:

— Ensure it is open and available for sale in your hotel or representation company's central reservation system (CRS) since the GDSs reflect the availability and rate data in the CRS

— Provide a full spectrum of public rates - rack, corporate, senior citizen, government / military, weekend and promotional

— Participate in consortia and negotiated corporate rate programs

— Ensure the room descriptions provided by the CRS to the GDSs are appealing, as well as accurate

— Periodically review the GDS property description for your hotel

The property description is frequently the only resource a travel agent reads prior to recommending a hotel to a client. Copies of the property description that appears in the GDS to describe your hotel can be obtained from the GDS database department of your chain or representation company. Use that same opportunity to request, review and revise your hotel's property description in the CRS.

Two further levels of GDS participation and promotion are available to you, one free of charge, the other at a fee. In the first, no-cost bulletin boards are available in each of the GDSs for posting announcements about promotional rates, seasonal packages and important news about individual hotels. These bulletin board announcements can draw travel agents' attention to your special offers. Contact your chain's GDS or electronic distribution department to inquire about displaying your hotel's information on these bulletin boards.

The second level offers a wide range of paid advertising options. Each of the GDSs have sign on messages displayed to travel agents as they begin their day, as well as numerous on-screen advertising opportunities tied to specific cities.

Internet Web Sites

Directors of sales often receive an average of one solicitation a day asking them to list their property on a web site. Evaluating the validity and value of those offers is often difficult. Web sites, like the GDSs, require several types of information in order to sell lodging – availability, rates and product description. In some cases, web sites link to existing sources of this information and need not be manually maintained by on-property staff. This is true of web sites for which data is provided by – or powered by – the hotel chain or representation company's central reservation system, a switch company or one of the GDSs.

Often the decision to participate in a CRS-, switch- or GDS-powered site is made at the chain or representation company level. In other cases, no arrangement or permission is gained. In some cases, the information is redisplayed by an associated onward distribution site. Onward distribution describes the process in which web sites repeat data maintained in another system or site. In most cases, this repetition is agreed to by the provider site. One example is Travelocity and its redisplay of Sabre's hotel and travel services data. Another is TravelWeb, who supplies its hotel data and booking capability to over 200 sites including CNNtraveller.com, Lastminute.com and Travelscape.com. In another much less desirable case, without permission a site screen scrapes information (sometimes only infrequently, resulting in out-of-date information being displayed) from a source site.

While individual properties have little control over whether they appear on these sites, since participation decisions are made at the corporate level, there often remains the opportunity to correct or enhance the data displayed. Periodically reviewing these sites will allow you to attempt to correct data displays that do not do justice to your hotel. Your chain or representation company's electronic distribution director should be able to supply you with a list of all of these sites which they are aware.

Web sites are no different from any other distribution or advertising medium in that they have specific user demographics. Site sales representatives should be able and prepared to describe those demographics to you. You in turn must decide if that constituency matches a priority market segment for your hotel. If a site is not powered i.e., does not draw its availability, rates and descriptive data from a CRS, switch or GDS, then the responsibility falls to the property to maintain the information on a day-to-day basis. This commitment cannot be taken lightly. Even the simplest of systems takes more time to maintain than the sales patter for the site generally suggests.

Some hotel staffs take the position that only occasional maintenance need be given, such as when occupancy begins to build they turn off these sites. In doing so, they shortchange a valuable opportunity for last room sale. This is occurring more frequently than most general managers and directors of sales are aware. The web site maintenance situation is improving, but widespread relief is months, and for most hotels, years off. PMS vendors are adding functions to allow a direct link to property web sites, so that a hotel can use its PMS as the real-time booking engine on its web site. Elsewhere, web site operators are beginning to develop PMS interfaces to allow automated downloading of Internet reservations to the PMS, and later, uploading of availability data. Additionally, master databases are in design, which will allow a one-time updating of a single master data file those updates will be instantly communicated to all of the web sites where you are listed.

Difficulties in first evaluating and later maintaining your hotel's information on travel web sites do not diminish their importance and a hotel's need to participate in them. The Web is quickly becoming a mainstream promotional and sales medium. It is essential to have a strategy for the extent and manner to which your hotel will participate in the Web and then the processes to ensure that strategy is applied on a day-to-day basis. Once your have chosen to list your hotel on a site, that and every other site where you are listed should be reviewed on a regular basis to verify that the data for your property is accurate, complete and compelling. If it is not, correcting the deficiencies needs to be a top priority. Next comes a commitment to maintain the same rates and availability data on the web sites as in all of your other sales vehicles – the front desk, the reservations office, the chain's reservations centers and the GDSs.

Differentiating the Web from the GDSs is the presence on the Internet of not only traditional "shop and buy" travel sites but also specialty sales sites. These sites, whose use may be appropriate from time to time by your hotel, specialize in selling distressed inventory. They operate using several models – discounted prices, auctions, reverse auctions and consolidators. Like the GDSs, web sites offer supplemental promotional opportunities. Preferred placement of your listing in sites or search engines, banner ads and additional on-screen graphics are just a few of the extra cost options.

As you decide to list your hotel's inventory on a site, inquire about the site's promotional possibilities. For the sites where participation has been arranged at a corporate level, ask the individual in your corporate office to provide you with a description of the opportunities offered by each of the sites. Electronic distribution and, in particular, the Internet is a complex and quickly changing sales environment. In the end, the powerful and productive sales tool called electronic distribution can be effectively employed because fundamental marketing principles apply to it just as they do in every marketing decision.

Electronic Payments

Before attempting to peer into the future of the dynamic electronic payments industry, one should first take a look back to examine just how we arrived where we are today. Five decades ago when the major card company's got their start, I'm not sure they had any idea of how pervasive the acceptance of credit cards would be in today's society. During the first two decades, the use of charge cards was strictly regional and based on relationships between banks and various "local" merchants. In the early 70's these issuing banks formed associations to enable cardholders to charge at any merchant's establishment, regardless of their banking relationship. At this time, card acceptance and accounting was a manual process, requiring merchants to deposit their charge slips as though they were checks.

The various card associations processed these cards by "key punching" them to paper cards and then onto magnetic tape. These card batches were then processed using the "big iron" computer hardware common to this era. This process was called the interchange, whereby charges made by the cardholders of one bank, could be transferred into funds to be deposited into the accounts of merchants of the local bank. This process took several days and delayed getting the merchant's money in their account. It was also expensive and that expense was borne completely by the merchant.

Acceptance of multiple cards at a single facility meant that the process and its inherent frustration were multiplied. The expense and delay of getting a merchant's money into the bank hampered the growth of charge card acceptance. Clearly, a method to quickly get these credit card transactions "interchanged" was needed. In the mid 70's banks formed independent third party processing companies who developed systems that connected the various bank associations, requiring merchants to communicate with a single entity to process multiple card types. Third party processors were a big stride in simplifying the interchange process. They gave hospitality merchants the ability to accept multiple card types through a single authorization and settlement point. The process at this point was improving, but the time to get the merchants' money into the bank was still an issue.

At the beginning of the forth decade of credit card acceptance, merchants demanded a faster way to get their money in the bank. To meet that demand, two companies created the first electronic credit card terminals. These devices have been the mainstays of merchant credit card acceptance for the last 20 years. With these powerful little devices, the third party processors are able to get the merchants' money into their accounts more quickly than ever. But with this speed, came the problem of fragmented deposits. This issue was most problematic within the hotel environment. A single hotel typically operates multiple profit centers under one roof (i.e. front desk, restaurant(s), retail gift shop(s), etc.) Furthermore, each of these entities could very well have multiple points at which credit cards are accepted. A single credit card terminal means a single deposit. Therefore, multiple terminals and multiple points of acceptance mean multiple deposits. This translates into more work in accounting to reconcile this mass of fragmented deposits.

By the early 90's many of the third party processors decided that they needed to provide hotel merchants with more efficient and convenient ways to handle credit cards. They created a technology that used the power of the PC located at the hotel property. Functioning as a hub for the multiple credit card terminals within a hotel, the PC-HUB consolidated each of the transactions before forwarding them to the processor, thus giving the hotel the speed of getting their money in the bank without the burden of increased accounting caused by multiple fragmented deposits. While many of the third party processors developed PC-HUB products of their own, First Data Corporation asked Shift4 Corporation to produce a PC-HUB product for them to sell. This started an entire industry of merchant centric credit card processing software to empower merchants rather than empower the banks, their card associations or even third party processors.

The last decade was marked by changing regulations instituted by the card associations. Again, the hospitality industry has lead the way in demanding advanced technology to help them meet these rules, in addition to meeting their needs for a faster, more efficient credit card acceptance process. This demand has lead to LAN-based credit card solutions, which interface directly to a hotel's PMS and POS systems. By providing a centralized point for credit card authorizations, settlements and accounting the directly interfaced, LAN-based credit card solutions saved money by reducing the need for phone lines from each point of sale. This move towards software-based solutions has all but eliminated the need for stand-beside credit card terminals

As the last decade of the 20th Century ends, the hospitality industry is again leading the way in pushing the electronic payment technology envelope. Hotel enterprises are demanding systems to process, not only credit card transactions, but transactions for private label cards including gift cards, stored value cards, discount cards, family cards, loyalty cards, and any other payment types. They want this functionality using their existing systems, no stand-beside terminals, without requiring a relationship with a particular bank or third party processor. Further, they are demanding systems that protect their entire enterprise from trusted employee fraud, and they want to get economies of scale when it comes to telecommunication functionality and charge-back defense.

Because the hospitality enterprise is often comprised of corporate owned properties and franchised properties, the proliferation of an enterprise private label system requires sophisticated technology. More often than not, hotel chains and management companies have different, competing merchant banking relationships. So looking to a bank or third party processors to provide this kind of multi-property system is all but futile. Private label programs require enterprise-wide systems that allow multiple POS devices to authorize and settle private label cards and standard credit cards using the same equipment.

By all indications the focus for hospitality enterprises is now on the customer. Added value and targeted marketing is the name of the game and the tools are quickly becoming card-based loyalty programs. But before card-based programs can spread their wings and fly, hospitality technology vendors will need to deliver advanced transaction processing systems and infrastructure to support these programs. Gift cards and stored value cards require real-time inter-property connectivity and centralized databases in order to track customer use while maintaining account balances and profiles.

Discount card and loyalty card programs are designed to track the purchasing habits of guests while at the property and follow rules defined to entice them to purchase products or services that the hotel wishes to promote. Again, inter-property connectivity and centralized databases are necessary. Family cards utilize rules databases to allow children or family members to share an account for purchases while on property(s). In order to make these card programs work across the multiple properties an enterprise-wide system is required.

With the technologies of the last decade, installing such systems was cost prohibitive and difficult to justify. With the advent of the Internet, a new class of application software is being developed; the Application Service. ASPs are emerging to meet the enterprise-level needs of hospitality companies. Application services are centralized server-based systems that use a company's wide area network (WAN) or the Internet to communicate to a centralized database, which serves dynamic application content to an end-user's web browser. These application services are typically less expensive to deploy than traditional on-site software models. In addition, such a centralized system can support private label functionality along with credit card processing. Further, when the card associations' regulations change, the hotel(s) bank changes, or the PMS/POS vendor(s) change, the hotel enterprise need only update the ASP server and every property is up-to-date the next time their users sign on.

The promise of this new class of system needs to be tempered with the understanding that these systems must be able to provide all of the existing functionality of the on property systems. Functionality like secure interfacing to existing property management and point-of-sale systems, secure communications with credit card terminals and the ability to audit transactions before settlement, archive settled transactions and retrieve archived transactions, all in real-time. All of this accomplished over the enterprise WAN, if available, or on the Internet, if not. Such systems should also be able to allow company web sites to securely accept credit cards to purchase merchandise, gift cards or for advanced reservations.

The hospitality enterprise is in the driver's seat. If they demand this technology it will become a reality. If the last 10 years of merchant-centric credit card processing software is any indication, it's just around the corner. A small company in Berkeley, California is paving the way for cardless and cashless payment at the point-of-sale—with more convenience to the consumer and many more benefits to the merchant than ever before. Introducing the next generation of electronic payment via SmartTouch Inc. featuring your very own unique fingerprint.

Let's talk convenience

Proponents of this technology praise it as a convenience paradise. Customers are freed from PIN numbers, cash, checks and plastic credit cards. Instead, a stored finger image is matched (or rejected) with the customer's and a payment mode (credit, debit, or ATM) is selected for a purchase. Once registered, a customer's finger image is stored and used for secure payment transfers at any participating POS. Molleen Theodore writes about this technology, "Increasingly, the way to keep information secure is to offer up a piece of yourself—a biometric identifier—to be recorded and used to verify your identity. Biometric identifiers are physiological and behavioral characteristics that are completely unique to you. "

Biometric identifiers work like this. With the SmartTouch fingerprint device, you place your finger on a scanner, also called a reader. A photograph of your fingerprint is taken, and software converts the fingerprint into a map of minutiae points—not the swirled lines we've all seen, but tiny irregularities within the print—which is stored for reference. When ready to make a purchase using the SmartTouch technology, a user holds a finger to the scanner, and the computer matches the stored print-map to the fingerprint. Only the minutiae points are stored in the image, not the actual fingerprint.

For merchants the benefits are just starting to surface. The most obvious include faster and more secure payments per customer. No longer will cashiers need to see identification or get a signed credit card slip because the scanned image is almost fraud-proof identification. Biometrics, because of their uniqueness to every person, are even more secure than current standards of payment. Improved loyalty programs are another interesting byproduct of this technology. Gone are the paper-punched-redeeming cards good for free sandwiches or sodas. Now with every customer purchase loyalty points or rewards are saved electronically and can be redeemed at the POS. Add to this the potential of using this technology for other things such as "keyless entry" for hotel rooms, paying for drinks at poolside or purchasing more credits at the slot machine, and you begin to see the scope of this technology.

With the touch of a finger a restaurant could in seconds have a payment of a meal, find out the customer's most ordered items and have the address of the customer to send out future coupons for their most ordered items. The restaurant provides better service and the customers receive their meals faster and are able to pay without paying. One of the benefits to the hospitality industry is in the cleansing of information.

Hotels are continually purging their records to keep accurate information on their guests (aka CRM). With the use of this technology a front desk clerk could know instantly at check-in that Mr. John Smith during his last stay purchased three Cokes from the mini-bar, two martini's in the lounge, ate dinner at the hotel restaurant where he ordered the special and since his last visit has moved from Chicago to Atlanta. All that from a fingerprint. Pretty amazing. And scary too. With all this information available and linked to a single image it is not difficult to understand why people are concerned with the potential uses and possibly misuses of this technology.

Biometric technology for payment processing has been in beta use for at least the past year, and SmartTouch has been working with a major US credit card processing company to prepare the technology for mass use. While the betas have been mostly successful there are no immediate plans to roll this out into the hospitality industry. Instead, the schedule is to introduce this technology to the multi-lane retail chains such as grocery stores and Walmarts/Kmarts within 8-12 months. But don't be too surprised if this new form of payment takes off once the masses are introduced to it and become accustomed to its convenience. Remember, it wasn't so long ago that the masses became accustomed to using a little plastic card.

With an infrastructure already being created, the price of the biometric sensors decreasing monthly and the given ease of retrofitting existing CC processors, this technology could be hitting the hospitality industry in a big way next year. There is so much more about biometrics to be covered. Consider this only a start. There are many proponents and adversaries of this technology, as it should be for any technology with such a wide potential for Hollywood-size disaster. Each side has valid arguments. The government thinks this is such an important topic that the legislature has been arguing both sides for quite some time.

E-business is defined as the transformation of key business processes through the use of Internet technologies. Most companies are looking at the Internet as a new marketing channel. You can find almost all the hotel chains, management companies, and individual properties on the Internet today. The chains are beginning to accept reservations directly on their web sites and are strongly encouraging customers to book via the Internet.

Many chains are also doing some type of auctioning for their unsold rooms. With all these online marketing tactics in place, many executives are now asking the question: "Are we making the most of our Internet strategy?" A critical element of this strategy should be how the company presents itself to its own employees, through the internal use of the Internet, known as the intranet. Most companies have implemented intranets, yet most have not realized their true potential in terms of cost savings, employee productivity, and business effectiveness. Companies are still sharing important business information with their employees by posting, copying articles, and passing information from desk to desk via a routing slip.

Very few executives have looked at the impact the web can have on reducing operational costs for the corporation. How many companies still print and mail policies to each location? How many companies still use dedicated communication lines to exchange information between properties and the corporate office? How many companies allow their employees to work from any location while traveling?

Cost reduction

In today's world, a hotel chain may reduce costs very quickly using the Internet. The Web can be the communication link between the corporate offices and the properties. Cable modems and ADSL/DSL lines are becoming available in many areas, replacing the dedicated phone lines of previous years. These new access and communication tools provide the bandwidth necessary to quickly move critical business information. There are some limitations on where these new devices can be used and when they will be available. The greatest limitation is the location of the properties and the speed with which the new services reach their areas. As these services become available, hotel companies need to review and adjust their telecommunication strategies.

While changing the circuits between corporate headquarters and a property reduces some costs, the real savings comes in reduced communication and administrative costs from using the web as the primary medium to communicate with employees. In the near future, this communication may include the use of voice over the Web. Some telephone/Web companies are offering this type of service today. Voice over the Web could reduce or eliminate both domestic and international long distance charges - a huge expense for any company. As an added bonus, the types of information that can be disseminated over the Web are virtually limitless: corporate policies, department information, and training to name just a few.

Corporate policies and information: Laws change frequently and corporations are responsible for keeping everyone current. This can be a daunting task for a small company, let alone a large company with hundreds of properties. The scope and flexibility of what you can do on the Web are truly remarkable. Here are just a few examples:

— share press releases,
— administrative policy changes,
— newsletters,
— company performance information,
— competitive information,
— new product information,
— new property updates,
— renovation/refurbishment plans and
— market information.

The beauty of the Web is that everyone can have the same information at the same time, regardless of where they are located.

Department information: Updated employee and customer contact lists, current financial, sales and performance statistics, near real-time sales lead status reports, resource availability, product development status reports, and marketing programs in progress all can be made available to your team members via the Web.

Employee productivity

E-mail and Messaging: The benefits of e-mail are obvious. Electronic messaging connects people who may be geographically dispersed, allowing them to conduct business quickly and efficiently across time zones. It can also be a vehicle for distributing and maintaining the corporate culture through near instantaneous communication of information, stories, and yes, even by supporting the ubiquitous grapevine?

Web Collaboration: Tools are now available that make it possible for people to share ideas and collaborate on complex projects by allowing people to participate from geographically distant locations. Team rooms can be established where central copies of documents are kept for easy access by all team members. Everyone contributes to the same copy of the document, which reduces errors and the administrative time needed to copy and distribute documents, receive and incorporate changes, then redistribute. Collaboration tools also facilitate workflow or the movement of information from one user to the next, based on guidelines and rules.

Training/distance learning: It's no secret that hotels have high employee turnover, making the time and cost to train and educate new recruits a substantial and continuous investment. Delivering training and other education over the Web will reduce both the cost and time involved and help new hires be productive more quickly. Sessions can easily be conducted on the Internet for new employee orientations, introducing administrative policies and procedures, conducting technical training on property hardware/software such as POS terminals, PMS system, word processing, spreadsheets, telephone system operation, or explaining new or changed governmental regulations on labor laws, environmental compliance, or foodservice. Travel and program development expenses can be significantly reduced using the Internet as a delivery mechanism.

E-HR (Electronic Human Resources)

This is one area where there can be huge benefits in automating processes and putting them on the Internet. Examples of e-HR applications include the ability to:

— Establish on-line employment applications; publish new hire checklists for managers;

— Allow on-line registration for health insurance; publish details on insurance benefit options and include searchable lists of approved facilities and physicians;

— Allow employees to register for 401K/pension program participation and permit them to view their accounts and change their investment options on-line;

— Publish bonus information, performance review criteria, organization charts and reporting chains;

— Publish travel expense policies and approved vendors;

— Allow submission, approval, and on-line lookup of expense reports and their payment status, time sheets, and tracking of vacations, holidays, sick and personal time, and

— Distribute electronic pay statements, which can replace paycheck stubs for employees choosing direct deposit.

Anything that doesn't require a personal presence can be conducted on the Web. With the advent of legally binding digital electronic signatures, even having to personally sign a form will quickly become a quaint custom from the past.

Business effectiveness

Business effectiveness boils down to doing the right things with a minimum of wasted effort. Easy to say, not so easy to do - at least until now. Internet technologies make it possible to do so on a scale unprecedented in history. Web collaboration allows you to apply your best minds to the project at hand, no matter where they may be. Real-time access to critical business information collapses the time needed to take advantage of market opportunities or head off competitive threats. Increased productivity is a natural byproduct of removing administrative and technical obstacles from employees' workflow. Reduced administrative head count and expenses allow precious profits to be directed to areas where they can generate the greatest return for the company. Indeed, using the Web for e-business from the inside may just be an hotelier's secret ingredient for marketplace success.

Timeshare Technology

Timeshare developers have sought distinction by routinely reinventing marketing efforts, inventory systems, contract terms, membership levels, and reservation policies. Until recently, many timeshare developers have found limited functionality in the marketing and management systems. Over the past 10 years, interval ownership has been one of the fastest growing sectors of the hospitality industry. Current sales levels are estimated to be over $3 billion annually at resorts located within the United States, while worldwide sales have surpassed $6 billion. Growth of the industry has been rapid, up more than 20 percent from 1994 levels worldwide.

Hospitality companies, land developers, and other entities are discovering that the interval ownership industry has developed and matured considerably, and conditions for entering the market are extremely favorable. The industry is now on a growth track that reflects the substantial acceptance among vacation and leisure-lifestyle consumers around the world. Despite its growth, the timeshare market has been somewhat overlooked and most likely misunderstood by many hospitality technology vendors.

As developers and properties have become more sophisticated, so have the amenities and guest service tools. Some companies are differentiating their timeshare products with spas, golf courses, restaurants, and retail. Owners at these properties expect the same ease of vacationing as they would from a luxury hotel, where they can move from activity to activity without reaching for their wallets. This requires well- integrated systems that combine member servicing and property management.

Timeshare system developers such as Resort Computer Corporation (RCC) have focused on the comprehensive sales and marketing tools, principal of which evolved from the real estate industry. Historically, the successful vacation condominium developer seeks systems to manage the voluminous tour flow of prospective purchasers while measuring the effectiveness of marketing programs. Second to sales and marketing is a robust receivables system that manages the many accounting functions of a timeshare resort.

A more recent challenge of interval ownership management systems is the transition to points-based membership programs. These programs have capitalized on the widespread acceptance of "points" as an alternative currency. Frequent customer and loyalty programs that reward users with points are offered throughout the travel and leisure industry. In the timeshare industry, members purchase an annual allotment of points used to redeem vacation lodging at affiliated resorts and clubs.

Not surprisingly PMS has been less relevant and in some timeshare resorts, continues to be a separate system or even a manual process. It is hard to say whether the timeshare development industry has been alienated by, or alienated itself from, the PMS industry, but the schism has been apparent as the hotel and interval ownership industries have begun to converge. Unlike traditional PMS software, timeshare inventory management is highly customized and governed by the ever-changing marketing programs. Many large timeshare corporations have spent millions developing their own systems.

Most companies rely on a hodge-podge of turn-key and archaic proprietary systems. New standards, however, are promoting the integration of highly evolved sales and marketing components with high-caliber property management systems and allowing a true customer-oriented resort environment. Many PMS products are simply not prepared to compete in the timeshare information management arena. Those that have proven themselves in the condominium and destination resort environment, such as Resort Data Processing (RDP) and Springer-Miller Systems are emerging as qualified providers to the burgeoning vacation ownership industry.

Springer-Miller Systems (SMS) and Resort Condominiums International (RCI) have strategically aligned to develop and integrate the products developed by RCC with SMS's robust resort property management systems. "By building on the powerful timeshare business logic that exists within the RCC system, Springer Miller Systems will offer a comprehensive management tool to destination resorts that include a timeshare component. The system will also be better suited for the stand-alone timeshare projects committed to a superior guest experience," said John Springer-Miller, founder and president of SMS.

The SMS alliance with RCI is anticipated to include central reservation interfaces with RCI's Global Points Network, an exchange system created specifically for points-based ownership programs. Vermont-based SMS has been serving the information management needs of major resort operators for two decades. The company has provided American Skiing Company (ASC) with CRS and PMS for a variety of lodging products including daily and weekly rentals, timeshare and whole ownership.

When ASC introduced the Grand Summit Resort concept at its most popular ski destinations, SMS demonstrated the flexibility of its PMS by accommodating the diverse usage patterns of a luxury quarter-share hotel. Each owner has 13 weeks of use, each of which can be reserved, placed in a rental pool, or exchanged through RCI. Due for release later this year is the fully integrated timeshare resort management system from CCS International, an affiliated company of Interval International. Resort Solutions will manage most aspects of timeshare operations— from lead generation, marketing, contract administration and commissions through member servicing, reservations, and resort financial management.

According to Assistant Vice President of CCS International Gene Pence, "The new system includes a sophisticated business-rules engine which allows the end-user to define any type of timeshare product, how it will be sold, and how an owner can use the inventory." The need for customized programming to accommodate evolving membership options is greatly reduced. Perhaps the most exciting feature of Resort Solutions is a central contact management database that allows any authorized user to view previous customer contact and account activity.

From a customer service perspective, having access to all databases is critical for efficient response and reduction of departmental workload. No longer do employees have to refer prospective leads or members throughout various departments in order to gather relevant account data. Recognizing the strengths of the existing property management systems developed for the resort hotel market, CCS International is also seeking partnerships for PMS integration.

The demographics of potential timeshare customers approximate those of frequent Internet users. A study conducted by Interval International in 1999 revealed that 88% of their members used a personal computer at home or at work. RDP, based in Vail, Colorado has been selling PMS solutions to a variety of timeshare concepts for 18 years. Founder Barry Biegler is quick to acknowledge the importance of Internet reservation capabilities for this market. Biegler said,"RDP offers 24-hour Internet reservation access allowing owners/members to make reservations at their convenience, and increase rental income for unsold inventory. Not only is room revenue maximized, but leads are generated and the cost of both transactions is greatly reduced."

Now more than ever timeshare and interval ownership developers require flexibility and scalability. The industry has rapidly evolved to satisfy consumer demand for flexible vacation options, yet the number of software and technology system providers has not increased proportionately. Alas, hospitality technology suppliers are seeing the untapped potential of the timeshare market. Partnerships between vendors will create "best of breed" solutions and the most well rounded of resort management tools. In the future, Hospitality Upgrade will report for timeshare decision-makers and the vendors who can offer them competitive technology products.

Evolutionary Nature of Technology

Improvements to a hotel's competitiveness yielded by technology are most often of an evolutionary nature, delivering benefits in relatively small increments that are quickly absorbed by a consumer directed market. The first hotel "business center" was homologous to the front desk. Occasionally the hotel administrative staff could be called upon to type up documents. Finer commercial oriented hotels offered a concierge staff to assist with professional services, either by locating a local merchant of secretarial wares or by commandeering a staff machine, and putting their own word processing skills to the test. For this level of service, the business traveler could expect to pay a premium for supplies and labor, not to mention a hefty tip

Soon these exponentially increasing requests began to take a toll on hotel staff, as well as hotel owned office equipment, without returning any significant revenue. The ever-diminishing front office labor model simply did not allow for this reallocation of minimum wage resources. Staffed business centers offered some relief, but minimal profit. Most hotels operated this department as a loss, but relished some marketing leverage and a perceived competitive advantage. Associated labor costs can exceed 75 percent of a staffed business center's revenue. Furthermore, these staffed centers are typically operated during "business hours" and certainly not during the "eleventh hour," when they are most sought after. In these scenarios, the burden of mass copying and collation is once again born by the solitary night auditor.

Today, various survey findings report that up to 85 percent of business travelers require the use of some type of office equipment while registered in a hotel. Nearly 60 percent of these travelers indicate that a hotel's ability to offer these services has bearing on their choice in accommodations. Even while claiming to be on vacation, 35 percent of professionals will seek the use of hotel business services at least once during the course of their repose. Rapid consumer acceptance of the recently introduced Wingate Inn (a Cendant brand) bolsters these sentiments. In addition to in-room amenities such as entertainment systems, cordless phones and high speed Internet access, every Wingate Inn hotel features a 24-hour access business center with free usage of fax, printing and copying equipment.

The Wingate strategy is a slightly higher room rate justified by an efficient working environment for the business traveler. The fact that these niche oriented properties are gobbling up market share from hotels that lack these office product offerings should serve as a wake up call to those who have yet to consider a self-service business center. Referring back to the "eleventh hour" phenomenon, it is important to understand that over 45 percent of business center transactions occur between the hours of 9 pm and 5 am.

Simply providing a computer workstation to your guests is a nice gesture, but requires some expertise on the part of the staff. Maintaining the equipment, the Internet connection for the various on-line services, the supplies, not to mention upgrades to software creates an additional challenge for untrained staff. The equipment is subjected to what can be a hostile environment and the supplies can quickly disappear into the brief cases of the less ethical.

Urban luxury and boutique properties are trending towards the in-room services and office prducts placed in each guestroom (or a portion of the rooms). Mid-scale and limited-service properties should look towards the increasingly popular automated, stand alone office systems to meet the needs of the traveling, working public. There are a growing number of affordable products being developed and installed as a convenience for the guest while creating a profit center for the hotel.

One form of cashless access to state-of-the art office products is made possible by TransAct, USA Technologies' patented credit card authorization technology. In a joint venture with Mail Boxes Etc., USA Technologies created MBE Business Express, an unattended, credit card activated business center, which allows a hotel to meet the copying, faxing and computing needs of its business travelers 24 hours a day. Each MBE

Business Express unit also features a dial-through telephone to a nearby Mail Boxes Etc. center for additional business, communications and postal services such as color copying projects, binding, packing and shipping.

Operating statements from comparable properties reveal that net revenue from these stand alone business centers contributes between one percent and two percent of the total property revenue. In some cases, this revenue per available room equals more than one half of that contributed by telephone revenue. Trends also show that the gap between these revenue streams is narrowing. Business center usage is clearly on the rise. Chief Operations Officer for USA Technologies, Steve Herbert, believes one of the most appealing aspects of the product is the ease of installing and maintaining the center. He said that "from a property perspective, they are hassle-free." Through a partnership agreement, IBM configures, tests, ships, installs and supports each unit.

Remote capabilities include troubleshooting and monitoring usage levels. Service and supplies can be dispatched from the same call center. Pricing for usage and output can be set remotely and increases consistency among properties of the same brand. The property pays a monthly service fee for the above and partakes in a percentage of the profits. The leading provider of in-room facsimile machines, AlphaNet Hospitality Systems, recently introduced The Office. In addition to "best-of-breed" hardware, popular business software and email access via major on-line providers, The Office also features turn-key Business Traveler Services.

Travel information, world news, financial information, sporting event and ticketing services are up front and convenient. Electronic concierge services will help eliminate the need for some hotel collateral material and calls placed to staff for local information. Direct marketing of other hotel services can be incorporated into the electronic display. Mark Holzberg, President of AlphaNet Hospitality Systems is particularly excited by the SmartCard capabilities of the credit card readers employed by his company's product. As more hotel companies launch sophisticated loyalty programs, value pre-stored on membership cards can be used to obtain business services, as well as rewards for frequent users.

With increased awareness of these capabilities comes increased need for secure card transactions. DJ Vallauri, VP of Marketing and Development, assures all users of The Office equipment's real time processing that reduces the risk of fraud and unauthorized use. The Office has a built-in remote monitoring system that proactively alerts AlphaNet's Customer Care Support Center of any potential malfunctions including paper jams. The creator of Business Anywhere, Kim Kao, describes an alternative technology that is employed by the Santa Anna-based vendor of audio visual and stand alone office products.

A patented fully interactive touch screen allows for the operation of up to 256 devices, including vending macines and video conferencing. Business Anywhere has recently been selected to be the sole provider of stand-alone business centers implemented in Hilton Hotels across the nation. The user-friendly touch screen is fitted with a single card reader, easy-to follow user instructions, and the custom splash screen serves as a marketing vehicle. This system separates the transaction processing from the functional equipment, allowing greater flexibility of product offerings, and concurrent use by multiple guests.

Open architecture allows for the ability to quickly increase the number of devices based on temporary volume. This would be particularly useful if a hotel expected increased business center demand, as a result of large group in house. Each of these vendors supplies an attractive, efficiently designed and placed workstation. Various financing and revenue models are available to meet the needs of the independent or chain-affiliated properties. We are entering the era of the fully automated hotel, connecting hotels and their guests to an expansive marketplace of diverse products and services offered by an array of providers.

There exists the possibility that some day technological innovations may actually reduce business travel. But as long as our guests are schlepping their laptops down the causeway, into overhead luggage bins, and up to our hotel rooms, we must be prepared to supplement their tools and support them in a world where commerce never sleeps.

Property Management System

Is it possible that in a few years hotels will no longer purchase property management systems? Instead they may point their standard Web browser to the site of their selected supplier, enter an account and password, and proceed with doing a check-in, folio posting, night audit, et cetera paying only a small charge for each transaction completed. If they change brand affiliation, or find a better applications supplier, the hotel could simply logon to a new Web site to begin service. This scenario is not realistic today but could become practical as Network Computing continues it's rapid evolution and many leading hotel companies and hotel technology vendors make plans to change the computing standards we now take for granted.

There are many types of technology in use today in hotels to provide property management functions. The majority are based on a local sever, a local area network (LAN), and either "dumb" character terminals or PCs. A very low percentage of worldwide installations are using a true graphical user interface (GUI) and only a fraction of these graphical systems are using a "thin client" or Web browser-based network computing architecture. Thousands of hotel properties will want to upgrade their PMS, and other hotel based systems, in the next few years to take advantage of the improved operations and functions available with a GUI. Network computing may offer them the opportunity to radically change the cost structure and operational requirement for hotel property automation.

Potential of Network Computing

There are a few important concepts in network computing. First is that the user terminal does not need to run a particular operating system, application, or even require hard disk storage. All data, business logic and applications reside permanently on servers and only information required for display is sent to the user device. Small applications or, applets, can be downloaded from the server and run in the local memory of the terminal to improve functionality or performance. There are several types of network computers (NCs) or "thin clients" but the most common environment for a networked-based application is the Web browser.

Web browsers run on many types of machines. They operate the same way regardless of which web application is running. Many workers are "pre-trained" on how to use a browser from use at home, and the bsiness application can be constantly updated and improved at the server, without ever having to upgrade or reconfigure the software on the client device. In a full NC configuration, printers and interface devices are also addressable by the host servers. While this architectural approach can be used within a single property, the real power of this concept is achieved when several hotels within a city, region, or country share application and database servers. Therefore for most hotels employing an NC option for PMS, these servers will be remote to the property resulting in a much simpler, cheaper, more reliable, yet more functional, systems environment.

The payoff for the operator of multiple sites is that only a single copy of the application and database must be maintained at the central location. There is no need to either visit a hotel, or download software to thousands of PCs, to update an application. This means systems organizations can be more responsive to business needs while maintaining a lower operating cost. If hotel chain operators or franchisers offered hotel applications based on web browsers, it could result in the ability to open a new property, or implement new functions, much faster and with less cost. This would make the brand more attractive, and raises the switching costs to move to another flag. On the other hand, if network computing becomes the industry norm, it could make it easier for hotels to change flags.

If a hotel chain can operate many properties from one shared services center, why can't a PMS vendor do this as well? The normal model for any hotel property with access to an external reservation source is to be connected over a wide-area network (WAN) to a remote application and database. This remote service is rarely owned by the property but instead they a pay a transaction fee for this service. The high number of transactions taking place within a PMS, and the high cost of telecommunication in the past, has kept the concept of the shared PMS from being widely used. Some vendors such as CLS and GEAC have offered this shared database design for many years but up to now, only offer this product for purchase by the hotel chain and only for character-based terminals.

The new economics of intranets, and the Internet, will make the concept of centrally - based computing feasible for technology vendors to offer transaction-based services to both branded and independent hotels. Think of some of the issues that would disappear if both the central reservation system and PMS were located at the same data center. Interface issues should not just be reduced, they should be eliminated because the CRS application and the PMS application could in fact be the same, sharing both business logic code and a single database. If a hotel were to purchase it's Information Processing requirements on a transaction basis such as per check-in, folio printed, occupied room, or guest check processed, it can save its capital for other investment needs and tie Information System operating expenses to actual use of the technology.

What does a hotel chain or technology vendor need to have to implement this network computing model? First, there must be a very robust application accessing a high capacity database. Although operating two-to-three hotels on one system has been done successfully by many chains, the shared system must support 50 to 500 properties to provide a profitable operaton for a vendor. There must be complete security and isolation of data between the properties yet the ability to provide consolidated reports for chain requirements. There has to be a physical data center staffed 24 hours a day with both technical and application support. It is important that the NC provider plan to offer as many of the current property-based applications as possible.

Many of the benefits for a hotel will not be realized if they eliminate the issues with PMS yet still must maintain existing client-server application on property for sales and catering, food & beverage, accounting, et cetra. Of course, there also must be a reliable network as this is such a critical component. Except for the smallest of properties, this would currently require the use of a private intranet. But as the Internet expands and improves, it will offer many more cost-effective communication options.

PricewaterhouseCoopers (PwC) conducted a short study of several large hotel chains and prominent PMS vendors to determine how much effort is being applied toward this architecture. Based on results of these questionnaires, network computing seems to have a bright future in the hotel industry. Seven of the largest international hotel chains were contacted to see what plans are being made for future property-based applications. There was near unanimous agreement on the following points:

— IT strategies include the use for more shared computing applications beyond the current examples of CRS, RMS, and accounting. This will hopefully include many PMS functions.

— The preferred user environment is clearly a Web browser.

— Number of properties to share a server or data center needed to be determined, but targets ranged from 30 to 500.

— Expected benefits include faster applications deployment, lower total cost of ownership, more stable applications, greater data integrity, more timely information when stored centrally, and a lower capital cost for hotel owners.

— There is no hospitality technology vendor today with proven solutions meeting these requirements, although several looked promising.

— All would consider purchasing these services on a transaction basis if the price and other factors were attractive.

The good news for all is that the technology vendors seem to thinking along the same lines. PwC also contacted seven of the largest technology suppliers to the industry with following results:

— All planned to offer, or have announced, new versions of their applications that will support multiple properties, sharing a server, and would be accessible using a Web browser.

— It was unknown at this time how many properties a single server would support but this would clearly vary based on the size and complexity of the properties.

— Most vendors planned to offer a native Web browser option by late 1999 or early next year.

— All the vendors agreed that network computing offered faster deployment of new applications and probably a lower total cost to the property.

— It is not clear, however, what the future opportunities are for supplying these services on a transaction basis. More than half of the replies indicated a strong desire to offer this service, but all agreed there were several technical, pricing, and operational issues to resolve.

The good news is that the PMS market has seldom seen such a variety of different approaches to solving your property's automation needs. The further good news is that the systems available have never been better for what is still the key system, the hub around which all other property systems revolve and in which you collect a huge amount of highly valuable guest data. The bad news is that you still have to make a choice.

The market at the moment can be summed up in one word - vibrant. There's a greater variety of offerings and more new ideas on how to use them than we've seen for quite a while. Windows-based systems have generally matured well and there are now several established, reliable and highly functional systems, usually based on Windows NT and SQL Server 7.0. But the more traditional systems with character-based screens are still around, and thriving. Whether running on DOS, UNIX or OS/400, there are plenty of choices, and they've been updated to suit modern demands. And the Internet is opening up all kinds of new possibilities for access to the systems and their data, possibilities that seem to expand every day.

Consolidation amongst the upper tier of vendors has resulted in fewer but stronger companies, while still maintaining a healthy level of competition. The mid-tier, such as MSI, RDP, Visual One Systems (formerly NGSC), HSS, Northwind and many others, continues to thrive, having expanded its customer base sufficiently to provide a solid base for growth. Increasing standardization of systems by the major chains - Fidelio/Geac for Starwood, REZsolutions/MSI/HSS for Cendant, Fidelio/HSI/MCorp for Carlson, Choice and Promus developing their own systems, and so on - seems to leave less room for the smaller vendors. Yet new systems continue to arrive, bringing fresh ideas and approaches such as Lodgical's focus on selling rooms by attribute, and Fabco's highly modular LodgeMaster, which offers a wide range of basic functions with in-depth add-on modules wherever you want them.

This is partly due to modern technology leveling the playing field and making entry more practical than ever for new developers. Windows, despite its programming complexity, makes it possible to create innovative, distinctive and intuitive user screens, and simplifies the integration of the PMS with office automation tools. Protocol Technologies' standard interface box provides an affordable, off-the-shelf solution for many of today's sub-system interfaces (point-of-sale, PBX, movies, credit card authorization, etc.), and HITIS continues to make progress in developing interface standards, which will be a boon for future developers. Standard report-generators such as Crystal Reports, and links to standard packages such as Microsoft Office, greatly ease reporting, in any custom format a property could want. And fast, reliable communications networks and remote-control software permit effective software support at virtually any distance from the head office.

The international scene is also flourishing, with several international vendors gaining significant market share in, for example, Britain (AremisSoft, InnSite), Europe (Hogatex) and Australia (CMS Hospitality). We found some exhibiting at HITEC, looking for partners and distributors to help them launch into the US market. Are they competitive? Absolutely. We live in a global economy, and in one of the most international of all industries. The major US vendors long ago learned that multi-country capabilities are essential to large-scale growth. The international vendors start with multi-country environments as their "domestic" territory. And don't forget that Fidelio, the largest PMS vendor out there, was a German company before being acquired by MICROS. Competition can come from anywhere, home or abroad.

So, the market is full of modern, attractive choices, almost an embarrassment of riches. You still have to narrow the field. Your first thought might be to focus on functionality. After all, the system must do what you need, at your property and in your environment, whether you have a 40-room resort or a 2,000-room convention hotel, though these will definitely have different priorities. But that doesn't really help to start with, but there are many different ways of satisfying similar operational needs, and most systems cover the fundamentals very well.

The "modern" choice; the combination of highly attractive user screens, widespread familiarity to the general population and a wealth of added functionality can make it seem almost automatic. But consider carefully before you buy. All those good things come with a fair degree of both technical and operational complexity, and you need to be prepared to commit resources to it to make it work well. What major benefits do hoteliers look for from a Windows environment? Those quoted most often are ease of training, ease of data transfer with other programs, and integration with office automation products (usually Microsoft Office). Yes, the systems are in general very satisfactory, the staff likes using them and likes their "modern" image. Yes, it is significantly simpler to set up data transfers between systems. Yes, they are easy to integrate with Office. And yes, they provide the power and flexibility for management to accomplish far more with them.

But like many powerful and complex tools, their benefits are only fully realized when you make a definite, committed investment in them, learning them thoroughly and making sure they're in the most productive environment. For example, Windows takes a lot of horsepower to run properly. This isn't a problem if you're putting in a new system from scratch; it's hard to buy a slow PC these days. But if you're upgrading to Windows and try to save money by running it on old PCs and networks, you'll regret it; it'll be slow and unreliable.

Windows systems are typically very flexible, and have many options - which gives you more things to learn and more ways to get lost. Good screen design can make a big difference in usability, though it's difficult to do well. Take the time to check that a potential system handles the key functions for your property unambiguously, and that it works the way you do. Each Windows system has a different character, just as properties do; make sure you get along before you commit. Despite these challenges, Windows systems have become well accepted and productive, as witness to their growing adoption by more and more chains. If you're at HITEC, check out HIS' Lodging Touch, REZsolution's GuestView, Eltrax's Medallion and HSI's Jaguar, all of which have received significant chain orders. Look also at the systems from smaller providers, especially those with a long track record with Windows systems such as Northwind's Maestro and VisualOne Systems' VisualOne, and those newer products from vendors with a long industry presence such as MSI's WinPMS, Fabco's LodgeMaster, Fidelio's Version 7 and Opera, and the British AremisSoft. And there are many, many other worthy systems out there.

But Windows isn't for everybody. Many hoteliers hold steady in their viewpoint that hospitality is still primarily a people business, and that technology shouldn't dominate. For them, it's important to have a tool that's capable, reliable and unobtrusive. One they don't have to spend a lot of time thinking about. They'd rather give their full attention to the guests and find that Windows systems require more time than they want to give. If you fall into this group, you still have plenty of choices among the character-based systems. A great benefit is that most have been around for quite a while, and have the full feature set that comes from years of steady development.

A long history usually also means that the vendor has worked out most of the bugs, and the systems are highly reliable. They're not necessarily the prettiest to look at; some make good use of color, some pack all those features into quite crowded screens. But they work and work well. They're up-to-date, too. The current release levels are all Y2K-ready, of course, and their vendors continue to release enhancements for such functions as Internet connectivity and data import/export. Eltrax, for example, recently released such enhancements for its Sulcus LANmark (DOS-based) and Encore Performer (Unix) systems. MAI's HIS keeps its

Paragon (AS/400) and CLS (Unix) systems current and reports steady demand for them, as do Fidelio (DOS) and Geac (Unix), still Starwood's two standard PMSs. And MCorp, which sells Northwind's Maestro in the USA, also continues to receive chain orders for its ImagInn (Unix) PMS.

The Windows movement will grow even larger as its environment and stability mature, and it's probable that many users of non-Windows systems are only waiting until their hardware investment has been more fully amortized before switching. More complex and demanding Internet-focused uses may at some point become more difficult to incorporate into the older platforms, requiring a shift to an alternative. At some point the vendors' installed base, especially of DOS-based systems, will shrink below an economic size to support. Although for now that still seems to be a few years off.

Unix and its headline-grabbing cousin, Linux, remain an interesting and viable option, although, unless Windows eventually implodes under the weight of it's massively complex code, one that is likely to remain in the minority. Originally designed by AT&T for communications purposes - almost all Internet servers use it - Unix is fast and stable, if not always the most intuitive operating system to work with. A number of very successful PMSs have been built on it - some listed above - and, while it does need it's own server, it can run on a standard office network without conflict.

Linux has gained widespread publicity and rapid growth as a cheaper and more universal option to the vendors' proprietary flavors of Unix, and is well-supported by a huge network of volunteers via the Internet. All HSS' current implementations use it, including the three thousand systems being installed in Cendant brands under the Power-Up program. Unix/ Linux don't exclude you from the attractions of Windows-like user screens, either, since X-Windows offers a very similar graphical appearance and usability. Although X-Windows has yet to appear on a PMS, HSS does use it for its back office accounting modules.

Thin-client computing

One of the hot buzzwords of the moment, thin-client computing is a modern version of the dumb-terminal environment (where all computing work is done on a central processor) but with full Windows capabilities on the terminals. These can be new, specialized units such as Network Computers, or older 386/486 PCs running under Citrix or Microsoft's Terminal Server software, which allow technically-obsolete PCs to run modern Windows applications. The superficial advantage of thin-client is that the hardware cost is lower, since the users' workstations can be simpler and less costly. They're smaller, too, since there's no processor unit, and this can help in tight situations. However, this is offset by higher central hardware costs, since the server needs enough power to handle every workstation and the network must have enough bandwidth to handle the much heavier traffic. Microsoft's per-station software cost is also not insignificant, and overall it often balances out.

The real advantage is one of control. Everyone is always on the same version of the same program, since they're all accessing the same copy on the server, so updating to a new version is a one-shot deal. And since there's no local disk storage, and no direct access to the Internet, non-standard programs can't find their way onto individual users' workstations. Not every program is a suitable candidate for thin client, but it can be worth looking into, especially for larger properties. Four Mirage properties in Las Vegas, for example, including the new 3,000-room Bellagio, use a thin-client implementation of Springer-Miller's SMS | Host PMS.

An extension of the thin client concept, "complexing" is the practice of running several properties on a single main processor, usually located in one property, with dedicated communications lines running to the other sites. Sheraton brought this to prominence as a means of sharing a Geac/UX PMS on a single Hewlett Packard Unix server between its three properties in Manhattan, and has extended it to other groups of hotels. Several other vendors have implemented these configurations where it makes sense for a geographical cluster of properties.

The Internet raises some interesting options, of course, here as everywhere else. Several vendors are looking at browser-based versions of their PMSs, which would allow remote users to access a central server using Internet technology. This may even lead to PMSs being available over the Internet from franchisers, or direct from vendors, to rent by the month to any property with a fast, reliable communications line.

Some complexing configurations allow each property to run entirely independently; others allow them to share rooms inventory and a single night audit process. Apart from the cost savings of sharing the server costs between locations, this also makes it easier to justify a central systems support group, leading to a better-running, more efficient operation for all. There are several other issues to keep in mind though. One is interfaces, since all POS, call accounting, movie and other charges from each property must find their way to the PMS server. And e-mail and other office automation tools may mean that you still have a server-driven network at each site. For properties already linked with a high-speed WAN, complexing can make a lot of sense.

Functionality

Following are the key functions that matter to your property:

— Are you highly group-oriented, and need very strong and flexible group booking/billing functions?

— Do you enjoy a high level of city-center convention activity and need powerful function/catering handling?

— Do you have a spa or many different guest-related activities and need a specialized module to track and bill them?

— Are you a boutique property that prides itself on outstanding service, and needs exceptional guest history features?

— Are you operating a roadside motel that just needs good, solid, straightforward guest handling with minimum fuss?

— Do a high percentage of your reservations come from a franchisor, a representation service or the Internet?

— Does the system provide interfaces to all the sub-systems you have on property and will not be replacing for some time?

You probably have a mix of these issues to deal with, but put them in priority and talk about those priorities with the vendors, and you should be able to reduce the system choices to a more manageable number quite quickly. Also ask some key questions of the vendor. How long have they been in business, and how many installations do they have of the system you're interested in and of all their products? How large is their support staff, and which of their customers can you call for references? Ideally, you could find the names of some of their less enthusiastic users, too - no one can keep everyone happy all the time - but always keep a sense of perspective about what you hear, from both camps. Their support needs are probably different from yours. When checking prices, don't forget to include all interfaces (these really add up), installation and training for your staff, annual service fees and any additional software needed to run the PMS, such as a database license.

Check on training, too, to make sure there's a balance. Too little is a waste of time and leads to frustration and inefficiency. Too much can be overwhelming, with the same result. Focusing on the essentials up front, and scheduling a return visit after a few months to build on them, is a better approach. Once again, when choosing between similar systems, don't underestimate the value of matching the system style to your operational style. A PMS is only a tool, after all, and a good tool feels instinctive in use, fading into the background and not getting in your way.

Hot functions that many hoteliers look for today include:

— *Full access to data*: This is becoming an absolute necessity, as the value of the guest and operations data contained in the PMS records becomes more and more apparent. Windows products make this easier, but most PMSs can import and export data in plain-character ASCII format with a little effort. Check how easy this is for the system you're considering.

— *Integration with Microsoft Office*: Almost a sub-set of the previous item. Many properties use standard office systems (of which Office has 90 percent of the market) for mail-merge marketing letters, spreadsheet analysis and graphical operational reports. Again, Windows-based systems have an obvious advantage but it's certainly possible in other environments. Ask for a demonstration.

— *Internet access:* Doing without this will get harder as travelers and businesses become more used to relying on the Internet, whether they're potential guests looking for information or reservations or suppliers offering discounts for internet-based ordering and settlement. Make sure your system can provide it, even if the way you'll use it isn't all that clear at the moment. Again, there's a caveat: security. Check for adequate safeguards on any external link, including passwords, encryption, anti-virus programs, firewalls and so on. And stay alert; both the benefits and vulnerability of the Internet change daily.

— *Revenue management:* More properties are aware of the bottom-line benefits that come from an awareness of each market segment's habits - when they come, in what quantities, and how far out they book - and in setting their rates and length-of-stay restrictions accordingly. In other words, aware of practicing revenue management. If you're seriously considering a full-strength revenue management program, because your guest mix is complex enough and variable enough to make it hard to track all the variables manually, make sure the PMS you buy has an RM interface, and a good one at that. If you're just looking to control fewer rate plan variables, make sure you're comfortable with the facilities built into the PMS itself. Many have surprisingly sophisticated and detailed options, while others take a less complex approach. There's a fine line between having enough options and having too many.

Hotel technology is often divided into three categories; technology for the guest, technology used internally, and technology that bolsters hotel relationships with the high tech world. Perhaps more than any other hotel industry supplier, electronic door lock manufacturers have demonstrated a commitment to each of these areas of product development. The evolution of the electronic door locking industry began with guest security, and expanded to increase operational efficiencies available to property management through access control and system integration.

The industry now stands poised to enter the new millenium as a major technology provider, positioning hotels as key players in an era of increased electronic commerce. Few inventions have had such widespread and practical appeal to the hospitality industry. Since the introduction of the recodable electronic door lock in the late 1970's, hotel security has been virtually transformed. The focus at the time of inception was increased guest security, but the benefit to the property was quickly realized.

Hotel security experts, along with media pundits, the courts, and the insurance industry all agree - keycard locks, which can be easily changed so that every guest gets a new key, are the best way to boost security. In fact, there is speculation that by the end of this decade, hotels that do not feature electronic locking mechanisms in guestrooms will be unable to obtain insurance. Even the simplest of key card locks have been found to reduce break ins by up to 80%, reminding us that effective guestroom security is an essential part of the hospitality package.

Employee access control was one of the first system enhancements to increase the level of internal technology. In order for a property to be maintained efficiently, hotel personnel require their own means of entry to rooms in which they must perform daily routines or tasks. In the past, distribution of conventional keys to housekeepers, room service attendants, and maintenance personnel compromised guest belongings and increased the liability of the hotel.

In some instances of theft, the victim was often the hotel (where even the negligent customer is king), and claims went unchallenged. The "burden of proof" is welcome by a hotel equipped with modern electronic locks, for the actual lock serves as a log, monitoring and recording up to 1,000 entries (about 100 days worth). Many reputations have been restored and many a thankful employee has been cleared of suspicion due to the success of these products. Employee key cards can be coded to allow access only to their assigned units of responsibility and only during the hours of their shift. Knowledge of these system capabilities may also serve as a deterrent to those less ethical.

Smart card technology

"Smart card" is a generic term for a card the size and thickness of a credit or debit card embedded with a microprocessor chip. The chip itself has intelligence and computational power similar to that of early personal computers. These powerful processing capabilities make smart cards much more secure than other types of cards presently in use. They can handle encryption techniques that protect the information stored on the cards.

A smart card as a very small personal computer belonging only to you. Because it's small enough to fit in your wallet, it's portable. And like a personal computer, it can be programmed to serve many different purposes and do many different things. Smart cards are currently being used to secure financial transactions, as stored value cards, for insurance identification, to store medical information and to personalize cellular phone communication from anywhere in the world. The beauty of the smart card is that it can offer all of these applications with considerable information storage capacity and security.

Phil Wilder, Director of Marketing for San Diego-based Computerized Security Systems, believes that the value added by smart card technology offers the hotel operator "a revolutionary new way of marketing and merchandising to the guest". In a world moving towards one-to-one marketing, smart cards hold the capability to customize and better serve individual needs. The smart card can carry information that is only yours, such as travel preferences and loyalty program account information. Programs and incentives are easily tailored to guests based on their own usage patterns of hotel services. Smart cards can also provide more privacy and security in accessing payments and information services, because the microprocessor chip that holds the information cannot be easily duplicated.

In July of 1998, Hilton Hotels International announced that the Hilton New York & Towers, the largest hotel in New York City, would become the first hotel in the nation to install a locking system fully integrated with true smart card capacity. There are an estimated 6,000 travelers who already carry credit cards with smart card technology.

Network and personal computer usage is one of the major applications driving smart cards, along with PCs, Internet access, security and financial applications. As more people utilize electronic commerce (shopping over the Internet), more secure methods of electronic payment will be demanded from these consumers. Self-proclaimed "futurist" Steve Hovanitz, Vice President of Sales & Marketing for Vingcard, envisions the following scenario made possible by smart card technology.

A business traveler uses his personal computer, with smart card reader, to buy an airline ticket and reserve a hotel room. Information transmitted through the Internet includes his frequent flyer number, as well as his credit card information to secure payment. Accommodation preference and loyalty program account information is also communicated electronically to the hotel booking service. Confirmation information is written to the smart card, and upon arrival at the airport, the card is used to obtain a boarding pass from an automated system.

Smart card is inserted to retrieve room assignment, secure payment, maybe even reward the loyal guest with a beverage value credited to his card. The same card is encoded with the room access information, and the card further serves as the key, allowing the guest to bypass the front desk entirely. Smart card applications heighten internal operational technology as well. Let's revisit employee access systems with Paul Zimmerman, Technical Director for North America at TimeLox. The world's largest hotel development to date, The Venetian (where else but Las Vegas), has just selected TimeLox to fit 6,000+ guestrooms and employee areas with the company's DC-One System.

The employee key card, traditionally identifies and controls access for authorized personnel; with smart card technology, the card becomes a walking production database. Reports generated from a maintenance engineer's smart card help verify work order fulfillment, by indicating whether or not a service call was placed to a specific room. Before the travel and tourism industry can see the full benefit of smart card technology, standards must be defined and upheld by the banking and software industries. It is important to observe that smart card technology may never take hold of our population, as it has in many European countries.

Information must be carried individually, because centralized data access and storage is not as reliable or efficient in other countries. The hospitality industry has historically been on the lagging edge of technology. From a service perspective, there has been a reluctance to embrace technology that makes any guest transaction less personal. Economically, the cost of keeping up with technology has often outweighed the benefits for an industry that relies so much on its human elements. The electronic locking industry is helping us transition, by incorporating new and exciting technology into an amenity that hotels cannot be without.

Electronic door lock makers are preparing for society's acceptance and increased reliance upon a technological prophesy that has yet to be fulfilled. However, proponents insist that the value added for consumers of these systems, is product readiness in a quickly changing world obsessed with convenience and security.

The Network Computing Alternative

Advances in network technology over the past few years have created an opportunity for companies to consider a new alternative for their computing needs. The use of wide area networks to connect company locations around the world has been in very limited use for many years. The most common example for these networks is hotel central reservation systems. Property management systems and accounting systems, the two most commonly used software applications in hotels, have mostly been property based, using minicomputers, local area network servers and desktop PCs as their hardware platforms. That technology model is changing today, opening opportunities that have not been either technologically or economically possible until now.

Today's wide area network is vastly different from networks of the past. There are many reasons for this, so let me mention just a few. Data transmission speeds have increased dramatically and the cost of increasing those speeds has significantly decreased at the same time. T-1 lines, once cost prohibitive to most businesses, are now relatively inexpensive. In addition, other options such as ISDN lines and "burstable" ISDN which allow even faster speeds have a significant impact on network justifications.

Telecommunications networks have been specifically created to carry data instead of trying to push data over voice circuits. And, perhaps as important as the improvement in network hardware, the almost universal accessibility to the Internet and acceptance of TCP/IP as the network protocol standard, as well as general availability of Frame Relay circuits around the world, has made network computing a reality. In addition, the sheer brute force power and reduced cost of modern computers, whether they be desktop systems, servers, minicomputers, midrange or mainframe computers has also been a major factor in making wide area networks possible. With all of this in place, a desktop machine connected to a network server thousands of miles away can have almost the same system speed and response time as if it were connected to a network server in the next room.

Network Applications

Another recent innovation is application software specifically designed for wide area networks. Perhaps the most innovative developments in this area have come from Citrix Systems, Inc. They are leading the development of server-based computing, using a relatively new concept called Independent Computing Architecture (ICA). This architecture is a three-tier, server-based computing technology that separates an application's logic from its user interface and allows 100% application execution on the server. In other words, the desktop device is simply a window into the Citrix server, which actually runs the program. Using powerful, but inexpensive, servers linked together as a server farm, the network operates much like a mainframe based system of 20 years ago.

However, there are some big differences. First, the desktop device can be almost type of workstation. PCs with as little as 8MB of memory and an Intel 486 chip can use this system. So can Pentium based PCs, inexpensive Network Computers (NCs) and, perhaps just as impressively, most MacIntosh computers. In fact, as long as the ICA client can be loaded on the desktop device, it will run the application. This is a real "thin client" opportunity. Second, unlike the mainframe-based systems, when a server fails, the other servers dynamically pick up the load.

At the same time, application developers have been creating versions specifically designed to work in the ICA environment. Although these are just coming to the market place at this time, they are worth serious consideration. Most developers working with ICA are taking existing, proven applications and modifying them for ICA. Applications not designed for ICA will not operate efficiently or may not operate at all. Initial releases of ICA compatible systems are mostly high volume applications, such as accounting, human resources, etc.

Yield Management System

When a hotel with an installed yield management system experiences in its first year a healthy growth in revenues from bookings, compared to the previous year when it did not use a system, who or what should get credit for the improved revenue performance? An argument can be made that the system really delivered benefits. However, the Sales & Marketing Department can claim that the new advertising campaigns and direct mail brought in greater volume. The Guest Services Department may claim higher guest satisfaction ratings generated considerable repeat business.

Considering all of these factors - and the activities enacted to affect revenue performance - one could even ask whether or not the yield management system is actually delivering benefits. Consequently, measuring the impact of the yield management system is essential to correctly attribute what revenue increases are a result of the system or are a result of other factors.

Plus, true system measurement is required for hotel owners and executives, who need to justify the purchase of the system, precisely understand return on investment, and prove system impact for a rollout. In the hospitality industry, there have been many approaches and technologies offered to provide yield management benefits. Likewise, there have been many attempts to help hoteliers see and understand what their yield management systems are doing for them.

Successful measurement can only occur when the hotel measures its performance working with the yield management system, and compare it to the revenue performance it would have received without the system, everything else being equal. Let's take a look at five of the more well-known measurement approaches.

The hotelier plots daily revenues from the past several years, and searches his or her findings for any type of trends. Spikes from the statistical noise produced from seasonality and demand fluctuations are smoothed to determine stable patterns. The patterns are used as a basis for making future projections, which are expected to grow at a steady rate. By comparing the future projections with any deviation from the projections, the amount of deviation, in theory, may be tied to the system.

However, this approach fails to account for the impact of new events that happened after the system was installed - new marketing campaigns or the introduction of a web site, for example - which were not done in the past.

It still makes it impossible to see what revenue change is due to the system or to other factors. A process is used to estimate what the unconstrained demand would have been or may have been. The process considers demand "on the books" and, after there is no more hotel capacity, it attempts to figure the amount of demand turned down.

With this information in hand, the hotelier speculates that, if he or she accepted the best business mix after the fact, how much revenue would have the property generated. That amount is compared to the actual amount of revenues. This difference or "gap" offers a possible measure for improvement. The "gap" before the system install is weighed against the "gap" after the system installation. The difference perhaps illustrates the system's impact. Simply, this approach only teaches the hotelier how to be wiser after the event, instead of making the best decisions for future booking opportunities. If you made investment decisions, in the stock market, for example, solely after the fact, knowing how prices fluctuated, and realizing when would have been the best time to buy and sell, you still would not enjoy optimum return because the decisions did not factor future volatility and uncertainty.

This approach can not separate what the system is doing and what is being affected by changing market conditions and other factors. In an attempt to estimate the yield management system results, revenues from a period after system installation are compared to a similar period last year prior to installation. To consider the effect of extraneous factors on revenues, the comparison is tracked against any demand fluctuations from a similar hotel (without the yield management system) in the same competitive set, and/or with nearly the same demographics.

Hotels and resorts pride themselves in their uniqueness. So it is impossible to imagine two hotels that would experience identical affects from the extraneous factors, and it is highly unlikely they would share the same pricing strategies directed or the same marketing mixes. Computer Simulation in Controlled Environments is vital that the system measurement is conducted in such a manner as to isolate the changes in market conditions and the business environment. One of the first places where this type of system measurement with isolation was attempted was in a controlled environment, using computer simulation.

In this case, a yield management practice with basic demand data is deployed. First, booking decisions from the yield management practice are based on simulated human decisions, which result in bookings accepted and not accepted. Next, the booking decisions are based on yield management system decisions. Again, bookings are accepted and not accepted. Accepted bookings from both decision scenarios translate into revenue, and the compared revenues between the two illustrate how the yield management practice may deliver results.

However, how can computer simulation understand truly how the humans would have acted? Humans are not efficient at executing on "first come and first served." Even if the measurement shows benefits in a controlled environment, how can the hotelier be assured that there will be benefits in the "real" world. It is impossible to predict in a controlled setting how the users would interact with the system. If demand does increase due to marketing programs or an improvement in economy after the yield system installation, occupancy will increase, and there will be more sold-out nights. But what if there is no increase in demand compared to last year, while an effective yield management practice is put into place?

As a result of the yield management system, it is anticipated that there will be a reduction in the number of turn downs multi-night stays. And the proper overbooking of rooms leads to a decrease in the amount of empty rooms on sold-out nights. Thus, occupancy will increase through the better yield practice. The scientific measurement approach is the tool with which it can be precisely determined whether the occupancy increased because of the yield management practice or due to marketing programs or improved economic conditions. It begins by identifying periods where the system does not restrict the hotel or resort in accepting bookings. This starts the process by which a look at what is occurring in the marketplace and in the local economy is gained.

Scientific measurement isolates the impact of the marketing programs and economic factors from the impact of the yield management solution. It shows what room revenue increases can be attributed to the yield management solution. Wireless or wired high speed Internet access ("HSIA") has become the new "must have" amenity for the business traveler in hotel public areas and guestrooms. Every segment of the hotel industry from Microtel to Four Seasons has recognized that business travelers want and expect access to Internet connections to handle work and personal matters while away from the home or office.

Currently, hospitality managers are not required by law to provide HSIA, whether wired or wireless, in hotel guestrooms or public areas. Hospitality managers, however, must provide an environment that is safe and secure for the patrons and guests while on their hotel or motel property. Once a hotel or motel provides a new service to its guests the law requires that they act prudently and use reasonable due care in providing and fulfilling the service. Generally speaking, the standard of care required by hospitality operators requires that a manager apply the same diligence as any other reasonable hospitality manager in a similar situation.

Standards of care are constantly evolving, however, reasonable care generally requires the manager to correct potentially harmful situations that they know exist or that may be reasonably foreseen to exist. For your guests' protection and your protection as a manager or owner of a lodging property, your guests need to know about the inherent risks in using HSIA in their guestrooms and in the public areas where wired or wireless service may be available. Once you begin providing HSIA services to your guests you are required to provide and perform the service in a safe and reasonable manner.

Here are a few suggestions that are aimed at protecting the legal liability of your hotel or motel:

1) Make it clear to your guests that the hotel does not directly control the Internet provider company nor the system providing wired or wireless HSIA to the guestrooms or public areas. Your literature or brochure describing this new amenity should expressly state that another company, independent from the property manager or owner, is providing the service and not the hotel or motel. Of course, you need to find a very

reliable source to provide the HSIA service to your guests; however, the guests need to be made aware that since you can't control the service, there is no guarantee.

2) It is critical that your Internet service provider or vendor goes through an extensive certification process whereby a complete security assessment is examined and security protocols are put in place prior to retaining them to install and provide the service. Don't use just any vendor to supply your Internet service. Do your homework and make sure that appropriate security measures are in place such as adequate firewalls and other features that are becoming standard in the industry for the protection of your guests and your hotel. You also want to make sure that the provider of the guestroom and public area HSIA system has security measures in place so that your own property management and hotel computer systems are not compromised in any way.

3) The Internet provider should include an on-line tutorial during the initial connection to the Internet whereby the guest must read and agree to the terms and conditions of use. The guest would be required to read through these paragraphs which will put the guest on notice of the inherent risks associated with using the Internet system provided. Providing notice of the risks is as simple as requiring them to electronically agree that they are aware of the significant security and privacy risks associated with accessing or transmitting information over the Internet, whether wired or wireless connections are used. Also include a clear disclaimer whereby the property and the Internet service provider are both protected stating

that they are not liable for any loss of data, file corruption, hacking or any damage to one's computer while using the Internet service. If the property allows the guest to print documents to a central printing resource in the hotel's business center or at the front desk, the guest needs to know that security, as to the contents of the documents, is not guaranteed.

The agreement must require that the guest accept the terms of the arrangement before logging on to the Internet. If an on-line disclaimer is not available, consider having your guests sign a written disclaimer prior to using the HSIA service. This disclaimer should contain the same items as described above. Make sure you keep the signed waiver on file in the event there is a claim brought by the guest in the future.

4) Your HSIA service needs to provide support for a VPN (Virtual Private Network) so that guests will be able to connect with their end-use home servers with confidence that security features are in place.

5) Ritz-Carlton has developed a concept called "Technology Butler" where by trained employees are available 24/7 to provide technological assistance to guests on various computer and Internet access needs. Other hotels and motels have or will most likely follow this service trend since guests will have questions about wired and/or wireless services provided in the hotel or motel and how to access the Internet. It is very important that a written procedure be created setting forth the rules for employees to follow when approached with a guest's computer needs request. Although not exhaustive of all procedures, such written procedures need to include, at a minimum:

— Untrained employees should never attempt to help a guest with his or her computer needs.

— Those employees who are trained to assist guests with technological needs should never personally touch the computer keyboard without the consent of the guest.

— The trained employee should keep the guest informed of every change to the computer settings or documents that will be made. Constant communication with the guest is essential.

— All employees assisting the guest with his/her computer needs must find out what the guest has already attempted to do up until the time that the trained employee begins to provide assistance.

— If the employee does not know how to solve the problem, he/she needs to call for assistance. No employee should attempt to do something on a guest's computer that they wouldn't do to their own computer. One simple error could be a very expensive one for your property.

— When possible, remind guests that wireless systems are not secure. Only non-critical email and basic Internet surfing should be accessed.

— Trained employees need to remind guests not to make any Internet purchases or do anything that could expose them to liability or potential identity theft, such as checking bank records or credit card statements, on wireless systems. The guest needs to know that a nearby hacker, who the property cannot control, may intercept his or her password and steal personal information of the guest.

— Be prepared to answer questions about whether the Internet sites visited by guests will be recorded somewhere on the hotel's computer system.

— Keep a detailed written log of all guest computer service requests including the date and time of a request, the guest's name, room number, specific request for assistance, action taken and the follow up with the guest.

— As more hotels and motels begin to provide, and continue to provide, HSIA systems for their guests, technology will advance and ultimately enable HSIA systems to be more secure. Meanwhile, take these steps to place your property in a much better legal position in the event something goes wrong.

Some hotels enjoy the revenue these special events provide to their properties with little or no concerns about disruption in operations. Others dread the thought of large groups of young people gathering in their lobby without any regard for the damage a can of silly string can do to a chandelier. Many hotel and motel managers are not aware of the laws that govern minor guests while on, in or about your property. The likelihood of loud disturbing noise, drug use and underage drinking should be on your high priority list. There are steps you can take to meet the needs of your underage guests while protecting your employees, other guests and your property.

Must you accept minor guests in your property? Generally speaking, the answer is yes. Innkeepers have a general duty to admit all persons who seek accommodations, unless the innkeeper has "just cause" to refuse accommodations. Just cause may include lack of available guestrooms, failure of the guest to pay for the charges and a reasonable belief that the guest may harm employees, other guests or your property. Failure to allow a minor as a registered guest in your property may be grounds for an unfair discrimination charge against the innkeeper. Since state and local laws differ, it is prudent for you to confirm your legal rights and obligations in your particular area with a qualified and competent attorney.

If you are fairly new to your property, find out all you can about the history of these types of events occurring at your property and surrounding hotels and motels. Does your property have a reputation that you would like to change? Perhaps tighter rules are in order or consistent compliance efforts are needed. Train your front desk in the proper procedures for admitting minor guests. Ask for photo identification. If the identification looks suspicious, ask for secondary identification. The Internet makes it very easy to obtain fraudulent identification cards.

All states prohibit underage drinking. An innkeeper can lose his/her liquor license and may be subject to liability for accidents that occur as a result of guests driving while intoxicated. Do not allow front desk personnel to give honor bar keys to underage guests. If your honor bars are not key controlled but are accessed through an easily breakable plastic ring, have all alcohol removed from the honor bar when minor guests rent the room. In addition, make sure alcohol is not delivered to guestrooms used exclusively by minor guests either through room service or as part of a frequent guest amenity program.

Anticipate the needs of small and large groups. Make it clear that guestrooms cannot sleep more than four people. Make sure you comply with your local fire codes on the number of occupants in the guestrooms at one time. Offer a hospitality suite or other meeting room space to minor guests late in the evening to lessen the chances of disturbing other guests. Add additional security measures on the evenings when your hotel hosts these types of events. For every group of fifty attendees, you might want to consider requiring the group to provide a security officer at their own expense. In addition, you may want to provide favorable room rates to parents in order to encourage the parents to stay the evening and chaperone the event. You may also want to provide, at your expense, additional security officers to walk the premises, including the parking lots, during these events. Make it known to all minors checking in to your property that security has been increased for their protection.

Make sure security is visible to the minor guests and that they know they will be observed. Providing notice in advance of what is unacceptable conduct or behavior on your property, coupled with a visible security team, will confirm to your minor guests that you mean business and intend to uphold the law. As an innkeeper you need to protect yourself from the risks imposed by a minor's legal status since a minor may revoke a contract and refuse to pay for room charges. Request that payment be made in advance either with cash or a valid credit card. Verify authorization of the credit cards used by minor guests. Verify ownership of the card and the right of the minor child to use the credit card.

Remind minor guests that disturbing noise, illegal drugs and underage drinking will not be permitted anywhere on the hotel property. As for intolerable noise levels, your rules may provide for an initial warning prior to any unregistered guests being escorted off property. Subsequent warnings will be grounds for the removal of the registered guests without a refund of the advance payment for room charges. Upon check in, a minor guest should be asked to provide parental contact information in the event the rules and regulations are not complied with during their stay and a call to the parents becomes necessary. Alternatively, you may request that the parent register the minor child or children so that the parents become aware of the rules and accept all responsibility for damage or injury during their children's stay.

Your rules may require that minor guests be required to sign a form upon check in acknowledging that they are familiar with the house rules and regulations and agree to comply with them during their stay. When you must take appropriate action to remove the guest, having a minor guest's signature on this type of form will help defeat the guest's claim that they didn't know the rules. Training your employees on these rules and regulations is also essential. Each and every employee needs to know the rules to ensure consistent enforcement throughout your property.

If you remove a minor guest from your property for failure to comply with the rules and regulations, you must exercise reasonable care. Depending on the specific circumstances, you may want to consider calling the parents or the police. Treat the guest as you would any other guest. For your guests protection and yours, don't let a guest who is noticeably intoxicated or under the influence of drugs to get behind the wheel of an automobile. Providing a safe, memorable evening for a young adult can create long term customer loyalty and possibly result in future revenues for other life changing events such as weddings, anniversaries, and the like.

5

Hotel Marketing

In limited service hotels, over 98% of the profit is associated with room revenues. In full service hotels, the corresponding figure is probably at least 80% and usually more, with few exceptions. While the importance of expense control in all areas of any hotel is critical to success, the fact remains that maximizing revenues is equally important and usually more difficult.

Expense control involves fewer people in the decision and subsequent action steps on a per dollar basis and the issues are usually more clear cut. Maximizing room revenues involves more people, in more subjective steps, for thousands of transactions (20,440 in a 100 room hotel with 70% occupancy and an average stay of 1.25 days!). Each of those transactions' value is at least equal to the average daily rate (ADR) and usually a lot more, depending on the length of stay. You could have several dozen employees at the front desk alone with the potential to make a significant impact on your room revenue. This staff includes reservationists, guest service agents , night auditors, switchboard/pbx operators and various supervisors.

In the case of the 100 room hotel above, assuming it has a $45 ADR, this would be room revenue of $1,149,750! And most of these employees are only paid between $1 to $3 over minimum wage. Imagine a 300-room hotel with a $65 ADR. Clearly, this is where the money is in a hotel; it's a hotel's reason for existing.

Some franchisors use discounting as the core of their marketing; one even tried to get their motels to sign people up for discounts when they were checking in with a confirmed reservation for a higher rate. No owner can take occupancy percentages to the bank to pay the mortgage, only dollars are accepted. Any time ADR is given up to achieve peak occupancy, money has usually been lost. Here is an example using our 100 room limited service motel for a year with a variable rooms department cost of $6.25: There are 25,550 occupied so the variable rooms so the variable cost cost is $159,687.50 is $148,281.25. Profit before departmental Profit before departmental fixed costs is $990,062.50 fixed costs is $1,002,381.30

Add into that savings on credit card commissions, franchise fees, wear and tear on rooms (maintenance) and energy and things really start to look better. This situation resulted in almost equal room revenue but considerably higher profit. Of course, you need to calculate what the trade-off in occupancy is and at what rate to improve profits at your property. Remember, occupancy is expense and ADR is revenue.

The point is that a properly trained and motivated front desk and reservations staff can dramatically increase a hotel's profitability. A typical hotel has five opportunities to establish the room rate charged the first-time guest:

— location;

— affiliation (or lack thereof);

— physical appearance and condition,

— the reservation process;

— and check-in.

These items might occur over time or almost simultaneously. The owner and management impact the first three while the front office staff have the largest impact on the last two. Yes, location can be improved by changing names (Days Inn Capitol Hill to Days Inn Capitol Downtown for instance), adding van service to one or two major demand generators or stretching the truth in maps and descriptive materials. The latter doesn't help repeat business, though. Affiliation must be appropriate to the market and the hotel's physical characteristics. The potential guests must perceive the condition and appearance of the physical facilities, particularly the exterior and lobby, to be equal to or somewhat better than what they are expecting to pay.

If the finishes and decor are much higher quality than they expect, they will be scared into believing the rates are higher than they actually are. Conversely, extra investment in guest rooms and in-room amenities will have a positive impact on repeat business. The owner and manager must give the front office staff a base from which to work on maximizing the room rates each day.

Even the simplest original design Super 8 Motel can offer at least two room types: a room with one double bed or a room with two of them. From that simple choice on, hotels and motels can layer on various bedding types, room sizes, locations, view and access. While construction and furnishing costs are almost identical, the room rating variations are larger. The room rating plan and related descriptions which are developed to appeal to the property's major customer types are one of the keys to increasing ADR at the front desk.

Here is a simple example of how this applies to an guest checking in with a confirmed reservation for the Super 8's room with one double bed: The guest service agent (GSA) simply offers the guest the room with two double beds so he or she will have more room to, "spread your things out." And the GSA points out that the double-double is "only $5.00 more". It is important to stress only the marginal additional cost. Clearly in a more sophisticated hotel with a concierge level, suites and king bedded rooms, the options are much larger and the opportunities to increase ADR easier. The point is, just because a guest has a reservation with a confirmed rate it does not mean an attempt cannot be made to upgrade the guest to a higher-rated room.

The real opportunities occur when people call to make reservations or walk in. In this situation, the first exchange with the guest is usually rate related. Instead, however, the pertinent questions at this point are really, "What dates would you prefer, for how many nights, and how many adults are in your party." One of the things a good reservationist or GSA will begin to discern from the answers to these questions is the purpose of the stay. This forms the basis for offering the guest the most appropriate room choices for their stay. Here it is of utmost importance to understand need/benefit selling and the concept of offering choices as a selling tool.

Need/benefit selling is simply the art of making a sale based on developing an understanding of the guest's needs and then subsequently offering the various room types not by just describing their physical characteristics but by translating those characteristics into benefits that might satisfy that guest's needs. The classic example might be offering a family of four two connecting rooms at a slight discount (single occupancy rate) rather than a double-double or offering a couple a king-bedded room. An obviously exhausted person might be offered a room with a whirlpool tub or a business person a room on the concierge level because it includes an honor bar and other amenities which are designed to appeal to those guests. Remember, these offers can also be made to a guest checking in with a reservation.

Another aspect in offering choices is how the rate offer is made. There are several techniques available for quoting rates and the appropriate one needs to be used for a particular guest. Some of the alternatives are:

— from the bottom up (that is quoting lowest first, then higher rates);

— top down (offering the highest rate and then backing off);

— or quoting the full range from bottom up and then repeating one, usually the middle one for emphasis.

Offering room and rate choices to a guest based on their needs is an excellent way for a reservationist or GSA who does not want to be a pushy sales person to really be the most productive sales person. If properly motivated and informed about the results, a front office team can have a substantive impact on room revenues using these techniques.

Room Keys and Security

Control of guest room keys is one of the cornerstones of what hotels must do in order to provide the safety our guests have a right to expect under common law. We, as innkeepers, have an obligation to take reasonable care that our guests will be safe in their rooms from intrusions by people who may have room keys. The following policies should be considered by all hoteliers who do not have key-card lock systems:

— Room keys must not have any form of tag which identifies the hotel or key blank which is particularly unique among the surrounding area's hotels. No key tag at all is preferred.

— Keys mustn't have the room number on them. Keys must be identified by a numeric or alpha code. That code cannot, in any way, directly correspond to the building or room numbers.

— When keys are given to guests at registration the guest's room number must not be said aloud if there are others in hearing range. Room numbers should be shown to the guest in writing with a reminder that they should note it if a guest check-in packet is not used. Explain to the guest that the coding system is for their protection.

— Guests should be asked for their room keys at checkout by the Guest Service Agents (GSAs). Hotel employees, particularly Housekeeping and Bell staff, who see guests who are obviously in the process of leaving the hotel for the final time (taking their luggage out) should ask guests if they have returned their room key. This is also a good time to thank them for staying with you and make other pleasantries.

— Room attendants and others who find keys in guest rooms or elsewhere should place them in their pockets or in the locked key boxes provided, not on their carts where they are accessible to others, and turn them into their supervisor to be returned to the Front Desk.

— All section masters, room masters grand masters and emergency masters, (normally kept in a safety box) should be signed out each time they are taken and their return noted. All of the keys should be stamped "DO NOT DUPLICATE." Persons who carry these keys should be spot checked to insure they have them on their person. The inspection is logged in the front office log.

— A record must be kept of how many keys are made for each room and when they are made. This record must be reviewed on a weekly basis by the General Manager. The General Manager must initial and date the key making log each time s/he reviews it.

— If indicated as a result of this review, the General Manager must instruct the maintenance staff either to rekey the lock or to exchange room locks around within a housekeeping section in order to save the expense of rekeying the lock. Numbers on keys must be adjusted accordingly and overstamped until the old number is illegible and the new number stamped nearby if locks are swapped in a section. As a standard practice it is recommended that some locks in a section be moved quarterly.

— A log must be kept of all lock swaps and rekeyings.

— If a section master is lost under circumstances which may result in our guests being at risk, the entire section should be rekeyed. If you rekey a section consider also rekeying to a new grand master and emergency master so that you are in effect beginning a phased rekeying of the entire hotel if it has been some time since this was done.

— If a master key or emergency key is lost under any circumstances it must be reported to the owner or corporate offices immediately by the General Manager.

After the circumstances are discussed, they can decide whether the entire hotel should be rekeyed.

As an additional step, the General Manager or somebody s/he delegates the responsibility to must cross index all incidents of theft, missing property, damage, etc. as follows:

— Room Number or Location. (Watch out for locks that have been moved.)

— Names of potentially implicated employees (usually more than one). You may discover that room thefts never occur when so and so is off or regardless of the room number so and so was working in maintenance or housekeeping.

Remember, you want to do your best to protect your guests by anticipating potential problems and want to protect your business by taking "reasonable and prudent care" and documenting your actions.

Safety Deposit Boxes and In-Room Safes

More and more hotels are either using in-room safes for securing guest valuables or even foregoing having safety deposit boxes available for guest use at all. This is creating some confusion as to how to take advantage of the protection hotels enjoy under Innkeeper's Law regarding the loss of guest valuables. In spite of the availability of the in-room safes, a hotel must continue to accept and deposit valuables and to be prepared to, "give the guest a receipt for them" (the valuables). The passive in-room system is not covered by Innkeeper Liability if the Innkeeper does not comply with Minnesota Statute 327.71 in its entirety. In other words, a guest who loses his or her property in the guest room, whether they use the in-room safe or not, has a claim against the hotel if the hotel does not comply with all the details of the law.

The Innkeeper's Liability Law must be conspicuously posted near the front desk and on the back of the guest room door in Minnesota. (Some states require the law to be posted in the room and don't say where and don't require it to be posted in the lobby.) Failure to post the law as required means the hotel foregoes the protection the law gives.

At some hotels with in-room safes, as part of the registration process, guests are asked to initial a stamped area on the registration card without explaining its significance. This stamp explains briefly something about the in-room safes and a dollar key charge or deposit. The hotel then adds a $1.00 per night charge for the in-room safe to the guest's folio. The typical guest would not carefully read or understood what they are initialing.

The initials are the vehicle by which these hotels obtain the guest's authorization for the daily charge. None of the stamps I've seen are worded as releases from the Innkeeper's Liability Law. These hotels are sometimes instructing their front office staff to tell the guests that the $1.00 is "security insurance". The term "insurance" has a very specific meaning and the application of this $1.00 charge for the availability of the in-room safes is probably not related to any real insurance policy. To say these safes are covered by insurance, if they are not, is misleading. To insure that the use of safety deposit boxes, in those hotels that have them, is adequately controlled, here are a few ideas to consider:

— File the box record (signature cards) with guest folios rather than in separate file. This will cut down on guests checking out and forgetting they have a box. It also insures that only guests and employees have boxes.

— File employees' box records with their personnel records. The General Manager or Controller should keep a current list of what boxes are assigned to employees.

— Keys for unused boxes should be kept in the Front Office Cash drawer or some other locked place, not in the key holes.

— Two or three employee safe boxes should be pulled and counted each month on a surprise basis to insure the boxes are correct and that no unauthorized items are in the box.

— Guests should be given privacy or a discreet distance when they are placing or removing articles from their box.

— If your hotel has in-room safes that you maintain a few safety deposit boxes at the front desk so, that in addition to posting the law properly, you will have fully complied with the Innkeeper's Law.

Taking Care of Travel Agents

Travel agents are an important source of business referrals for many hotel properties. To maximize this source, eryone should treat travel agents, and the business they refer, in the best possible manner. As a major potential source of business referrals, travel agents must receive a commensurate amount of attention from the hotels to which they refer business. The three most important things to a travel agent are:

— Ease of making reservations with confidence.

— Client (guest) satisfaction.

— Prompt and accurate commission payment

General Rules General hotel procedures to remember to get the most out of this business:

1. Never dishonor a reservation made by a travel agent.

2. Clearly note on each reservation, registration card and folio that the guest was booked by a travel agent. This is best done by obtaining a rubber stamp, "TA," for this purpose.

3. If a travel agent uses your hotel regularly, be sure to tell their clients at check-in that you appreciate the fact they booked through that agency and that you think very highly of that agency. Leave a small gift or treat for them occasionally, compliments of the agency that booked them. They'll appreciate it and their thanking the agency will get the word to just the person you are really trying to please.

4. If it won't cost the hotel any revenue, upgrade the guest to a better room and advise the guest you are doing it because they used that particularly agency.

5. Keep a list of reservations booked by agencies and use them to learn:

   — Agency productivity

   — Recent bookings

   — Frequent guests using a particular agency

   — Frequency of bookings by a specific agency

6. Use this information in your marketing efforts. On a periodic basis (at least quarterly) the travel agent

payment files should be reviewed so that targeted marketing can be developed to further penetrate this often essential source of business.

While having a policy of never dishonoring a travel agent's reservation, it is also very important to make sure they can communicate with the hotel with ease and that they have a good point of contact. Ideally, this could be the Front Office supervisor in a smaller property.

In a larger property, it might be both the Reservations Manager and someone in the Sales Department. These people should visit with the agents booking the hotel on a regular basis at least quarterly just for the sake of having personal contact or bonding a little. Thank you notes and other gestures are always welcome with the booking agents and agency managers. For chain affiliated properties, it is important to insure that the hotels' data is accurately reflected in the various airline reservation systems used by the travel industry. Stop by a travel agency where you have contacts and ask them to show you the hotel's displays. Usually, the chain's headquarters can also provide copies.

Always pay travel agents as soon as possible. The goal should be paying on a daily basis. This is only possible if the hotel has someone at the hotel with the authority to write these checks and is truly only feasible if the hotel has more than 120 rooms with sufficient travel agent volume to justify the steps. The following are suggested procedures for smaller hotels paying on a weekly basis:

1. Each day have the night auditor list the checkouts, if any, of guests booked by travel agents. The list should include:

   — Guest's full name, room rate paid, arrival date and departure date.

- — Agency name, agent's name (if available) and complete address.
- — Your calculation of the 10% commission due on room charges only.

2. Each Thursday, the Front Office Supervisor (or General Manager for a smaller property) should review and sign the list as authorization for your central office, General Manager, or your Accounting Department to pay the commission. The reviewer should check the list against actual folios on a frequent but irregular basis.
3. Your central office, General Manager, or your accounting department should pay the commissions as soon as the list is received on a weekly basis. Consider including a hotel brochure or some other promotional piece with the checks when they are mailed.

Adopting a "Pay Travel Agents Today" program can be well worth the effort. It is designed to address the prompt and accurate commission payment issue often complained about by travel agents across the country.

1. Each hotel should operate a separate checking account for commission payment purposes only with the following specifications.

- — Authorized signatures - Front Office Manager, his/her supervisor, Controller, General Manager, company president.
- — Checks should be marked "Not Valid For Over $50.00" (or the maximum reasonable amount for your hotel), have vouchers and be two-part forms.
- — The balance in the account should normally not exceed one week's average commission payments. Verify the amount with your Corporate Office.

— The bank statement should be mailed directly to the Corporate Office or your accounting department if all bank reconciliations are done on the property.

2. Each night, the night auditor should list the previous day's checkouts on which a commission is due and leave the list for the Front Office Supervisor.

3. Each morning the Front Office Supervisor will pull the folios from the night audit packet and copy, then return the originals to the packet.

4. The Front Office Supervisor should prepare checks payable to the travel agents in the appropriate amount.

5. A check register should be completed and a copy of each folio should be attached to the register. The copy should be annoted with the check number and date.

6. The check should be mailed that day with the voucher portion clearly showing the guest name, dates of stay, room rate commission amount and the name of the booking agent, if available.

7. Each Friday the check registers and the supporting folios must be turned into the hotel's controller, or to the Corporate Office if your hotel is on centralized accounting, along with a check request. He/she will review the documentation and, if all is in order, will immediately reimburse the account for the amount spent with a check payable to that account.

8. The copy of the check/voucher retained by the Front Office Supervisor should be filed alphabetically by agency name in reservations or at the front desk.

Adapting these ideas to your hotel will help increase travel agent business over time.

Hotel Marketing through Internet

Hotel bookings through the Internet, whether on franchise web sites or electronic distribution channels, have risen exponentially. As reported by Travel Click in a recent article in Hotel Online, GDS bookings increased in 2003 3. 3% while the Consumer Internet Channel bookings increased by 34. 7%. This has led many hotels and hotel companies to re-allocate sales and marketing resources to managing and manipulating their positioning on the Internet. They are quite correct in doing so — this is a trend that is not only not going away but will continue this kind of growth for at least a few years into the future. This percentage increase, unfortunately, has not been characteristic of most hotel sales departments and, as a result, the precious marketing resources available to them have, in many cases, been reduced to accommodate the expenditures on Internet channels and web presence.

As a result, many hotel sales people have become frustrated and discouraged to the point that they wonder if there is a continuing role for them as this trend continues. The answer to this question is a qualified "yes. " The traditional methods and modes of conducting hotel sales will not produce the results that will alleviate this concern. It is a simple case of "if you keep on doing what you have always done, you will continue to get what you have always gotten. "

In today's environment, that leads to diminishing returns as travel and meeting planners turn to the Internet more and more to evaluate rate and amenity positioning prior to ever contacting a hotel. Often, the second step is to visit the web site of a particular property, again prior to contacting the sales department. What can sales departments do to increase productivity, avoid becoming an in-house amenity or, the worst possible case scenario, the dinosaurs of the industry?

Hotels need to include the sales departments in their Internet positioning and web design so that the message and offering is consistent across the customer touch points. In addition, sales departments need to embrace the technology and use the Internet to become more productive and efficient in conducting hotel sales at every step of the sales process. For example: Target Market Prospecting In an attempt to locate new markets as existing ones are producing less, the decision is often made to target markets that previously were ignored. This can range from government (all of a sudden per diems don't look so bad from a rate standpoint), SMERF, Affinity groups, etc.

Traditional Sales Locate existing or dead files for prospects in these target markets then begin contacting them one at a time. If they weren't producing before, why would they now and how long will it take you to contact enough prospects in a new market to ascertain its depth? Cyber Sales Conduct a web search that becomes increasingly specific until a prospect list or database can be located on related web sites. Market Penetration Strategy In most cases, it is impossible to ascertain the depth of a market or begin to penetrate it without making contact with a significant number of prospects. How to do this efficiently? Traditional Sales They are still contacting the "dead" files.

Contacting one individual or organization with a phone call is very time consuming and not very efficient. Cyber Sales Develops an email postcard or an email message with a benefits tease, copies and pastes email addresses into a group on the email address book, puts each name on the email as a bcc. and sends it off to groups of ten or twenty at a time to avoid the appearance of "spamming" with the ISP. Initial Approach The name of a prospective organization and key contact information is available.

Traditional Sales Pick up the telephone and call them. Upon routing to their voice mail, leave a message with your name, the hotel's name and phone number. Cyber Sales Locate the e-mail address on the web site or call the central number, press zero (normally there is still a human available) and ask for the contact's email address. A recent client was absolutely amazed at how willing the receptionist was to give out the email address. This is only a brief glimpse at how hotel sales departments can incorporate the Internet into their every day activities to contact more prospects more efficiently.

Each of the examples above are just the beginning of the techniques that hotel sales departments can use to incorporate the internet into their activities to penetrate target markets, develop new prospects and maintain relationships. People are now used to initiating and building business relationships through email, instant messaging, etc. Once we have "touched" them enough times electronically, it is then possible to make a telephone appointment to build on the relationship. A telephone appointment is more efficient than leaving voice mails. The message here is that hotel sales departments can use the Internet in many ways to become more productive and efficient.

In spite of more rapid growth in other parts of the world, notably in East Asia & Pacific and the Middle East, Europe retains by far the greatest hotel capacity of the six worldwide tourism regions, as defined by the WTO, with about 6.2 million rooms. Overall, Europe's hotel stock, differs fundamentally from that existing elsewhere in the world in that, for the most part, it consists of older, and, on average, smaller units. The European hotel sector is also far more fragmented than in most other regions worldwide.

In Europe only about 20%-25% of room capacity is branded by an integrated chain, (i.e. not including consortia), whereas in North America approximately 70% of the hotel stock is chain-managed or franchised. The rest of the world falls somewhere in between these figures. Within Europe, the degree of chain penetration varies greatly by country. Basically, countries with large nationally based chains such as France, UK, and Spain have higher levels of chain concentration than countries where the roster of locally based players is limited to small and medium-sized hotel groups as in Germany, Italy and Switzerland.

Paris-based Accor dwarfs all other hotel operating groups in Europe with an estimated 20% of chain-operated capacity in the European Union. As the fourth-ranked hotel company in the world by number of rooms, Accor manages the two biggest brands in the area; Ibis, Mercure, as well as Novotel, Formule 1, and Etap which are in fourth, sixth, and tenth position respectively. In addition to the brands mentioned above, Accor has an upscale flag, Sofitel, and a new extended-stay product, Suitehotels, which has just begun operations in the Paris and Lille metropolitan areas.

Of Accor's 440,807 rooms worldwide at end 2002, 51% or 225,284 are to be found in Europe. Over half of the latter number, or 116,118 (52%) are located in France. In spite of this concentration in its home country, Accor is the number one hotel operator in several other European nations, including Germany, Belgium, Switzerland, Hungary, and Poland. In March of this year, the former Six Continents split into two separately quoted entities InterContinental, plc, which owns the hotel brands (Holiday Inn, Express by

Holiday Inn, Crowne Plaza, InterContinental, and Staybridge Suites), and Mitchells & Butler, which has taken over the group's restaurant and pub activities.

Société du Louvre, a publicly quoted company controlled by the Tattinger family (the Champagne producers), combines both upscale hotels with its Groupe Concorde, and budget hotels (Groupe Envergure.) Hilton Group, plc is a British-based chain which has the rights to exploit the Hilton name outside the USA, which is the province of Los Angles-based Hilton, Inc. The only thing that links the two Hilton's is a worldwide marketing agreement, as the two entities remain entirely separated as to ownership.

For the average independent European hotel, the best affiliation solution is often to be found with a voluntary chain or consortium. These two terms are basically synonymous and refer to loosely structured hotel groupings, which demand less of the individual hotelier in terms of conformity to rigidly prescribed standards, and, especially, in terms of costs. Whilst the independent hotelier can pay as much as 7% to 10% of his annual rooms revenues for an integrated chain brand franchise, such as Holiday Inn or Ibis , voluntary affiliations typically cost much less - between 1% and 2%. In fact, yearly franchise fees charged by an integrated chain often represent only the "tip of the iceberg", as compared to the total outlays necessary to renovate and maintain a property to the chain's standards.

Another advantage to the hotelier is the ease with which the affiliation can be cancelled, usually within a period of two years or less, as opposed to chain franchise or management agreements which typically stretch over decades. In any case, the great majority of independent European hotels are unattractive to the major "hard brand" chains due to being too small, or having the wrong location. Integrated chains favour properties having at least 50 rooms and located in urban areas or nearby transportation arteries such as motorways or airports. Thus for all the above reasons, a voluntary association frequently best meets the needs of the independent European hotelier.

For instance, in Switzerland, a country notorious for its highly fragmented hotel sector, an estimated 27% of total rooms capacity is affiliated to a consortium, whilst only 8% of rooms are branded by an integrated chain. Elsewhere, voluntary chain associations are well-developed in France, Spain, and Germany, although no precise figures exist as to penetration of the overall hotel stock. Whilst consortia and representation groups have been typically structured as not-for-profit associations, organised on a country-by-country basis, there is a trend, particularly in the upscale segment, for them to become profit-making enterprises. For example, Leading Hotels of the World, Relais & Chateaux, and Indecorp have been incorporated as for-profit entities.

Best Western, for instance, has announced fourteen new operating standards, covering such basic items as requiring coffee and tea making facilities, hair dryers, and ironing boards in all guest rooms to free local phone calls and data port connections, which were to be respected as of the beginning of 2001. Best Western has yearly inspections and even Logis de France with almost 4,000 hotels has one person who visits each new affiliate's premises. Relais & Chateaux has ejected 161 properties which failed to meet its increased quality standards.

6

Effective Branding

In the hotel industry, renovation has come to mean "reinvention" — with observers pointing to soft sales as an opportunity to not only make needed improvements without displacing as much income, but also to rethink their brand and market niche. Part of this effort has come to mean design standards that far more subtly reinforce the brand and at times means introducing new brands for national chains that want to target specific and very narrow market segments.

Branding expert Michael Salius of Boston-based Pirozzolo Company points out, "A hotel brand must have a distinct promise, character and personality that evokes expectations and an emotional response from the target market. It must also convey, a valuable single nugget size idea to those whose business you solicit. Look at successes outside hospitality: Volvo promises — and delivers — safety, Maytag promises and delivers reliability — With Southwest, 'You're free to move about the country. '"

Every hotel operator must ask: "How is my property different from my competition and which of those differences are important to my target market segment. And every designer or hotel executive in charge of design standards, must ask how well does the design reinforce those differences and giving them credibility and depth that goes deep into every fiber of the property.

A half century ago, and with budget hotel chains today, the challenge of national branding is relatively simple. Red Roof Inn for example adopted Howard Johnson's strategy of being identified with its roof and tedious consistency. Among higher end properties the major chains still want to build equity in their national brand but their individual properties must now be distinct, harmonize with their geographic location and resonate with the values of the target market. And, the trend is toward slicing the market into increasingly narrow segments.

Hilton, for example, has established distinct brands for Hilton Hotels, Hilton Inns, Hilton Corporate and Hampton Inns. Another contemporary approach is to create a stand-alone brand. For example, the goal of Marriott's Renaissance Hotels, is to establish a distinct Renaissance brand not, say, Renaissance by Marriott, as with Courtyard by Marriott. Teri Urovsky, vice president of interior design for Marriott Hotels & Resorts, to describe the role design plays in establishing the Renaissance brand; which targets an upscale businessperson who enjoys the travel experience. Says Urovsky, the Renaissance brand is based on three principles: savvy service, street level restaurant and expressive design. Based on these principals, location plays a big role in the way the property is rolled out to the customer. She says, "Every Renaissance hotel tells a distinct design story. In Niagara Falls it is an upscale couples' retreat based on the fantasy of travel. " The theme is reinforced with design elements such as a leather steamer trunk in the lobby, frosted globe lighting fixtures and guestroom corridors done in a color scheme based on the Canadian

Mounties uniform, known for its red tunic and brass buttons. Individual guestrooms are Moroccan in tone.

The Renaissance hotel offers a Kodak moment, e. g. a place to take pictures such as a grand stairway that places the property in its locale. Every guestroom has an impressive headboard feature using rich materials such as leather and exotic woods, a living room atmosphere in the lobby and a library-like bar or lounge. Colors are warm, rich, and vibrant and color combinations are contemporary. Particular attention is paid to all lightning — both ambient, and direct as well as the lighting of artwork and artifacts.

One attribute of Renaissance that introduced in numerous properties is a human scale front desk/ welcoming point that allows the attendant to step out in front and relate with guests without a barrier. After all, Front desks no longer need to built to hold guest mail, hang keys and support a ledger-size guest register. They do need to be designed to establish a relationship between the hotel and its guests that is positive and sets the tone for the entire stay. When it comes to interpreting national design standards at the local level, the Newport (RI) Marriott stands is a superb example of how our firm capitalized on its Newport location while still communicating the Marriott brand identity. For this property, we retained the art director from Jurassic Park to create a soaring sculpture made up of colorful sails for the lobby atrium. This and other oceanic themes — including sculptures of the Greek god Neptune —let guests know they are in the land of the America's Cup. At the same time the sophisticated look is unmistakably Marriott.

In the past, a few overarching visual cues could be executed cookie cutter fashion to support a hotel's identity, today's interior design must still reinforce the brand, but must do so subtly with each element woven into the fabric of the property. To make it all work we abide by three principles.

— Never resort to clichés or a one-size-fits-all design solution that does not fully reinforce the hotel brand and the needs of its market.

— Never place the designer's vision ahead of the owner's but instead fully research the hotel's brand and determine how it is being supported in every aspect including not only design standards but operations as well.

— Always be on the lookout for new products and design ideas to enhance your ability to visually reinforce the brand with originality, impact, depth and superb taste.

Hotel Broadband Market

The hotel broadband market has experienced a considerable recovery over the past year and is positioned for further future growth, reports In-Stat/MDR. The high-tech market research firm reports that, despite the downturn in the travel industry, hotels now perceive broadband as a necessary service offering to remain competitive in the current environment. As a result, there has been a significant shift in the market from being a service provider driven one to what is now a demand driven business, both on the part of the guest and hotel.

"Hotels are acting on the new vision of broadband's importance to their competitive ability, and more and more properties are offering high-speed access as an amenity," says Amy Cravens, a Senior Analyst with In-Stat/MDR. "This renewed strength in the hotel broadband market will be reflected by an increasing number of rooms deployed each year."

In-Stat/MDR has also found that: Although there are considerable regional differences, hotels worldwide are following this trend. While North America leads the worldwide market, Asia Pacific also represents strong opportunity. Europe has been a slower market in the past, yet In-Stat/MDR expects considerable growth in this region in 2004.

According to an In-Stat/MDR survey, over half of the respondents indicated that the hotel owned the network equipment, illustrating a significant adoption of this new model. Hotel ownership of the equipment, and the broadband service, creates a more stable operating environment for the providers, as well as allowing the hotel more creativity for pricing structures—some even making the service free, as the Marriott chain has recently done.

The emerging new business models are also capitalizing on the introduction of new services and applications. Simple service offerings, such as creating a printing network, which link guestrooms to a central printer, are emerging, as well as more complex offerings, such as Video-on-Demand (VoD). Networks are also being viewed as operational tools. For instance, branded portals act as a virtual concierge for in-room services, as well as a marketing device. Some hotels are even envisioning creating "smart guestrooms," where environmental controls and other in-room devices are linked to the network.

7

Travel Guidance

Some companies already have that position and most should, especially now that the economy is dictating a move away from accounting driven corporate cultures to sales driven cultures. Most hotels went on 'auto pilot' when the summer season approached and made certain that the revenue management systems were in place to maximize the revenues generated by peak demand. Although drive markets continue to feel the least pain, air travel, while increasing, is expected to be well below the previous two years and this year's traveler is looking for value in all areas of their travel arrangements.

While the General Manager has always been the CEO of their hotel – to their staff and to their customers — most have yet to truly use the power of the position effectively to promote sales and assume the role of CMO. General Managers who rose through the ranks on the operations side are now under increasing pressure from their corporate office to become actively involved in the sales effort. GMs that assumed their positions during the 'boom' years excel at revenue management but are unsure how to support and monitor the sales effort. Those that remember the last economic downturn have in many cases forgotten how to do that.

Market intelligence or Market IQ is something that the GM is in a unique position to gather. Do you:

— Attend planning and zoning meetings

— Schmooze the Economic Development people (they do use your hotel when they bring in prospective company's executives, don't they?)

— Participate actively in industry associations

— Browse the business section of your local paper every day – bankruptcies generate a lot of business

— Visit your fellow GMs and make a mental note of who is doing business at their hotel that day

— Network with consultants (like me) and the business reporters of your local papers to get a broad overview of the market

A part of developing your Market IQ is to truly appraise your property in relation to the competition. Have you evaluated the strengths and weaknesses of their department heads and your buddy, the GM? Ask a friend to stay at their hotel one weekend with a checklist from you to get a perspective on the guest experience at your competitors.

When was the last time you picked up the phone and asked a guest or a corporate account contact "How well are we serving you?" Do you know not only the names of your top accounts but have you had lunch with your top account contacts? Do you have your own contacts at that account, one step above the contact of your sales department?

Your top accounts, contacts and guests think that you are the CEO of the hotel – you have the power to make anything right! Use the power of your position to assist in the sales and marketing effort. Become the CMO as well as the CEO!

Hotels often brag that they are running 100% market share penetration. If a property is positioned well in the market in terms of product and rate, 100% market share is what you get for opening the front door and not chasing customers out the back door with poor service. Over and above 100% is the result of an effective sales effort.

For example, a client said to me recently that the bad news was that one of his hotels was $50,000 down for the month over the previous year but the good news was they were running 117% market share and 125% Yield index. In markets that are declining it is still possible to run well above 100% Market Share so eliminate the excuse that declining market share is a function of a 'bad market'. A simple definition of 100% Market Share is that if your hotel accounts for 20% of all available rooms in a market and you received 20% of all occupied rooms in a given time period, you achieved your fair share of the occupied rooms or 100% of your fair market share. This appears on your Smith Travel STR reports monthly.

However, you who may not have access to that report because you are in a small market that does not have enough properties reporting to Smith Travel to constitute a statistically valid competitive set or because you are not franchised or operate in a market with many independent, non-franchised hotels. In those situations, it is still relatively easy to calculate market share if the other properties will share their occupancies or if your area has a lodging tax. On the contrary, the opportunity to manage the revenue in order to maximize the Yield Index occurs when a hotel is running above 100% Market Share.

At less than 100% Market Share, it is difficult to pick and choose clients who fit your ideal client profiles (you did develop those didn't you after reading last month's article in this publication?). The hotel is accepting the business that comes to it rather than developing business that will be the most profitable for the property. Going out and actively soliciting business is key to market share penetration. In any given market there few, if any hotels, that have their sales people out on the street asking for the business. The sales team will not totally know which clients fit their profiles without qualifying all of the businesses or organizations within their market. It is just as important to understand who does not have business for the property, as it is to know who does.

A lot of time is wasted pursuing clients that have no potential for the property. That is a result of poor qualification techniques. Once you have identified a prospect that you think may have business for you, do your homework. This is so much easier now with the resources available on the Internet. Log onto what you think may be their web site address or do a search. This will give you valuable information on the organization including the size, locations, mission statement or value proposition as well as key contacts.

In some cases, especially with associations, it will also give you information on where they held their last meeting and annual conference. The location and the hotel that was used will tell you if they are in your 'ball park'. Going into an appointment prepared will impress your prospective client and give you some insight into how to approach them. The following are some of the questions to ask during the qualifying process:

— Do you use hotels in the area?

— Who in the company (organization) makes decisions about hotel selection and reservations? How much time is spent talking to someone who has no decision-making authority?

— Which properties do you currently use for your transient and/or group business and how many rooms do you use over the course of a month or a year? This will tell you a lot about their rate sensitivity, the amenities that are important to them and potential volume.

— Why do you use them and are you happy with the way they are serving you? This question will give you insight into the 'hot buttons' or buying factors that are key to closing the account.

— What rate range do you look for in selecting a hotel? You probably have a good idea on the answer to this one from the above questions but it will tell you if they have a negotiated rate at your competitors, that is, if you know your competition's rate structure.

— Many people in your local market may not have been to you property recently or at all. You may have renovated or made significant improvements since they last saw your hotel. Don't assume that they know your product or your rate structure.

You may only have one chance to see this contact, make an impression and begin a relationship that could lead to new business for your hotel. The answers that you receive to the above questions will allow you tailor your property presentation to the prospects 'hot buttons' or the things that are important to them in making a hotel selection. The key to a successful property presentation is to know your presentation so well that you don't have to think about what you are going to say next and not to dwell on features that are unimportant to them.

A wise man once said that a rising tide floats all boats. In most markets the tide is going out and not rising. Those properties that don't mount a skilled and effective sales effort will find themselves beached. Attaining market share over 100% is about rising above the tide.

The initial reaction on the part of hotel managers and sales staff is to shrug their shoulders and blame it on the market as though they have little control. The inevitable result of that attitude is to find that you or your hotel is on the block, as some managers and sales people with Adam's Mark are about to discover. This transaction is only the tip of the iceberg. For those companies wise enough to retain some of their profits, the time has never been better to acquire hotels. During the last eight years, demand was sufficient that many sales departments of hotels, CVBs and other tourism related industries responded to inquiries and decided whether the piece of business fit their revenue parameters.

Sales people and managers need to rediscover the art of new business development or prospecting. In deference to those sales people who entered the industry within the last decade, many of them don't know how to find new business. They are named the 'dead files' for a reason and the ratio of time expended to business booked is not a profitable percentage. Most wise managers and sales staffs have strategically redistributed their percentages of business per market segment to reflect current economic conditions and not past history. This means that if your local corporate market is down, reduce that percentage and replace it with groups or individual leisure. The discount segment right now is exceeding projections made prior to the economic downturn, which means lower average rates but potentially higher volume. The first step is to decide who your potential clients are in all market segments if calling efforts are to be maximized. In these economic conditions, the call to closing ratios have increased tremendously. It pays to have sales people and telemarketers calling on qualified lists of prospects.

Take the time to develop a 'client profile' for each market segment that you want to solicit. The client profile is composed of the following elements:

— *Geography* – Where do your clients in a given market segment originate? This information may be available through your franchise SOB or feeder market reports. Audit the existing files for that segment and tally up their markets of origin. Are your clients for this segment national, regional, intrastate or local?

— *Demographics* – What is the size of the average company, group or tour that currently uses your facility? How large a group can the facility accommodate? In order to maximize the utilization of the function space, what is the size and configuration of the ideal group? Is most of your group business corporate, association, SMERF or leisure? What mix of those segments represents the maximization of revenue? Does your corporate business originate with Fortune 100, 500 or 1000 companies? What is the demographic of your leisure business – families, seniors, DINKS?

— *Fiscal Profile* – What rate does your ideal client want to pay? How flexible are you on rates on a case-by-case basis? What is your preferred form of payment? Does your ideal client pay their bills on time? What value can you add to the package for this client that can justify additional rate? What additional value-adds or features are they willing to pay a premium for?

Until we know who we are looking for, it is difficult to go and find them. Many lists are available but they need to be 'sliced' by the parameters of the 'ideal client' profile. There are few things more discouraging than to have a relatively inexperienced sales person (and we never assign this task to the sales people with seniority) cold call on a list that is not qualified. After the first several hundred calls with no firm leads, they become pretty discouraged.

This is the strategic first piece of the process. Once the profiles have been used to slice the lists and target other prospecting activities, the rest is dependent on training in the rest of steps of the sales process. Taking the time to develop an ideal client profile for each market segment will save time and energy in the long run as your calling efforts will be targeted. The ideal client profile should change with time as economic and market conditions change. The properties goals and objectives change. However, without a client profile you are shooting scatter shot into a flock of ducks hoping to hit one. With a client profile you are aiming and shooting at a specified target.

Nothing can approximate the loss and sense of grief that we feel for the victims of the World Trade Center and the Pentagon Tragedies. However, the economic aftermath is just beginning to take shape and it is ugly. Now, the most patriotic thing that we can do for our country and ourselves is to get back to business and try to stabilize this economy. Most of you have just finished or are in the process of completing the marketing and business plan for 2002. 2001 has been difficult for an industry that was posting double-digit gains in revenue for the better part of the last decade. According to PKF the average US hotel will suffer a 5.6% decline in operating profits in 2001 compared with a 10% increase in profits in 2000. That was written prior to September 11, 2001.

Many hotels and hotel management companies are ill equipped to deal with this sudden turn of events. Demand has been so strong for the last ten years, we have focused on managing yield rather than generating demand. Demand has not slowed down, in many market segments, it has come to a screeching halt. Most impacted are those convention and meeting hotels with long term bookings that are suddenly cancelled until further notice. Corporate travel, even if the fear of flying did not exist, will be impacted by the airline's curtailment of 20% of their schedules on average. How deeply and for how long leisure travel will be impacted is anyone's guess. Life as we have come to know it has come to an end, at least for the near future.

Everyone is now the competition. From the limited service franchise down the street to the luxury hotel at the other end of the street. Don't hold on to a rate structure that has you positioned in your 'market/product segment.' It is war out there. The client doesn't care about your rate position in your market segment – they care about value and service for their scarce travel dollars. Do what it takes to retain your current accounts and steal new ones.

If your top accounts are leaving you for the limited service hotel down the street, drop your rate and build in breakfast. If you have a food and beverage outlet, throw in a coupon for a free beverage. Offer an incentive to use the restaurant for meals other than breakfast. Will it reduce your overall revenues — maybe. If your clients leave you for the amenities that your competition includes in the rate, your revenue will most certainly be reduced even further.

Reduce your projections by a minimum of 20% across the board for the first six months of the year (and that is probably optimistic). Target those with which you can realistically have an impact and solicit like crazy. Some of those include government, drive-in markets like AARP and AAA. Develop packages for those guests that may now arrive by rail. Develop local 'vacation' packages for those in your area and within drive proximity that won't be flying this year. Remember, SMERFs and Associations have members not stockholders and may be inclined to continue their activities at a reduced budget closer to home. Go after those small accounts you couldn't be bothered with last year – the last economic recovery was built on small businesses.

Resist the urge to cut the A & P budget. Don't throw your money away on any advertising or promotions that can't be tracked and evaluated as to direct revenue produced. Do use your budget to keep your frequent guests in your franchise loyalty programs close to you. Build in value adds to keep them from going down the street. Advertise only in vehicles proven to be effective – if an ad rep comes to you make them show you their numbers, the results produced for other clients in the industry.

Resist the urge to cut the sales staff. Recruit additional staff from the competitor down the street who's stealing your accounts. Train them – remember, many sales people for the last ten years have been answering the phone. Train them to prospect and sell, then reward them with incentives. Maximize the franchise resources that you have at your disposal. Instead of grousing about how you are not getting a return on your franchise investment – work it. Participate in all the programs that make sense for your market. Call your franchise services marketing managers and seek their advice.

Use the national sales office resources to facilitate access to national accounts. Access the databases of your franchise loyalty programs to formulate cost-effective methods of promoting and communicating with your customers both present and past. These databases contain an incredible amount of knowledge about your guests. Develop your own Customer Relationship Management program.

Now more than ever, focus on the GSAs and their customer service skills. Train your managers and supervisors to train them on the nuts and bolts of delivering good customer service. We have been cavalier about our customer service during the period of time when demand was high. Who cared if we alienated a few guests – there were plenty more waiting to get in. Going the extra mile was the exception rather than the rule. The NYC police and firefighters have offered us a hard lesson and a wake-up call – the extra mile is the only one that matters.

It is time to get back to our 'core competencies' in the hotel industry, as Carol Walter and Mark Haley alluded in their article of September 14 in this publication. We have become asset managers, real estate companies and statisticians. While all of the above have their role and none of us intentionally operate non-profit organizations, we have lost our focus. It is no longer 'build it and they will come' – it is now how do we locate potential guests in a contracting market, how do we persuade them to come to our hotels rather than the competition and once there, how do we keep them coming back.

A very wise and prominent man in our industry, Bob Alter, President of Sunstone Hotels once said' "It is easy to bring the dollars to the bottom line when you have them coming in on the top line." During the recession of the early 90s, he focused on the sales effort at his hotels and they were ahead of the curve when the economic recovery began. This should be self-evident, but is it truly sales and customer service that drives your hotels?

All organizations reach a point at some time when they are aware that they could be doing things better or differently. One or several areas of the operation are not achieving their goal or are not functioning as efficiently as they might. The Corporate Office, General Manager and the Department head may aware of the problem but unable to offer or formulate an effective remedy. This is where the timely employment of a consultant can reap measurable returns. The issue or problem may be short-term. For example, a property or a group of properties may be undergoing a franchise change.

To effectively manage the change and maximize the opportunity will require an intense effort, analysis and focus that will stress the existing organization's resources and potentially jeopardize the well being of the rest of the operation. This is a situation where a consultant can assist in managing the change until the conversion is complete and the newly franchised properties have stabilized. Another example is when a position is stubbornly vacant and the right candidate has yet to materialize or the position is such that it can be effectively filled on a part-time basis. To leave the position vacant is hurting the operation but to make a hasty decision has long-term consequences. This is an illustration of how a temporary arrangement with a consultant can keep the operation moving smoothly until a position can be permanently filled.

In other situations, the issue may be more long term and the effective use of a consultant on an ongoing basis may be a cost effective solution to the problem. For example, a smaller organization may not have the resources of a larger company in oversight or training. The list of potentially problem areas is relatively endless and includes any number of operational, technical and customer service areas. A good consultant-client relationship is a professional marriage. A consultant wants to provide value to the client but recognizes that it requires a bit of work on both sides.

Once you have identified one or more consultants who may be qualified to assist you in your problem area, have a telephone conversation with each. As is any relationship, chemistry is an issue. You know if this is person has a style that will compliment and mesh with yours and that of the people in your organization. Not every client and consultant has the chemistry required to get the job done, no matter how qualified the consultant. Ask for references and examples of how they successfully assisted other clients in similar situations.

Most consultants are willing to do this for expenses or a minimal fee. A good consultant is set of 'fresh eyes' – someone who can give you an objective opinion of the elements of the situation and recommendations for a resolution. However, resist the urge to 'shoot the messenger' if their analysis does not exactly agree with your perception. Some clients simply want an echo of the conclusion they have already drawn to validate their own opinion.

In many cases, the consultant is a small business operator and invoices left unpaid for over thirty days puts him or her in a bind and gets your account poorly served. The single most frustrating thing to a consultant is a client with whom the chemistry is right, the terms of contract are clear but the client does not implement or support the agreed upon action plans and recommendations. The consultant has no authority to enforce the performance of the action plans except the authority and express support that you give them. In those situations where everyone loves the recommendations and action plans but there is no support for their implementation, the consultant invariably gets the blame for poor results. It's your money – use it wisely.

— *Agree to Disagree on Occasion.* A good consultant is there to stimulate you and provide another opinion. If everything you were doing in the past was so good, how did you get into this situation in the first place? If you keep on doing what you are doing you will keep on getting what you've gotten. A disagreement on an issue doesn't mean that you are wrong. Back your ego out of it and be willing to listen to a dissenting opinion. At least agree to think about it.

— *Commit to the Agenda.* A good consultant will furnish you with an itinerary prior to the visit and it is up to you to ensure that the staff involved has cleared their calendars to give the consultant their focus and attention. A consultant's time is very expensive to waste. A staff member who is feeling threatened or defensive will often avoid spending the required time with the consultant. While a good consultant will try to put their fears to rest (unless they are the problem), it up to you to make it clear to the staff that the consultant is there to identify and support solutions, not to threaten or find fault. However, as the saying goes, if you are not part of the solution, you are part of the problem.

— *Communicate, Communicate, Communicate.* As in any good relationship, success depends upon the level of communication between the parties involved. Make sure that the staff provides the reports the consultant requests. A good consultant will begin their itinerary with a meeting with the key contact(s) and conclude with the same. Read and share with the staff the report that the consultant furnishes after each visit and discuss on the phone.

A good consultant is not someone who is 'between jobs' or unemployable. Most have held positions of responsibility and produced results for their employers. That is how they developed their expertise. They are doing what they do for various reasons and not looking for a job. A good consultant has usually been offered numerous jobs by clients but prefers to do consulting for the challenge, variety and flexibility that it affords.

A good consultant is a consummate 'hole plugger' and problem fixer that can generate many times their fees in additional revenue provided that you, the client, know how to use them effectively.

Hotel's Economic Landing

In US, the Federal Reserve planned for a 'soft landing' of the economy, the 'impact ', however, has been softer for some than for others. Those hotel sectors most impacted are those that were in areas dominated by tech companies and extended stay and limited serve products that were in overbuilt markets. While pilots say that 'any landing you walk away from is a good one', merely surviving isn't sufficient for owners who have been used to double-digit revenue growth for the last five years.

Given the rising cost of energy, that puts many hoteliers at a deficit even if they just maintain current market share. The summer of 2001 will probably hold challenges that many hotel managers and sales departments haven't dealt with before. Instead of managing the yield produced by high demand they will need to generate demand from market segments impacted by lay-offs, high gasoline prices and declining disposable income from deflated stock portfolios. Generating demand is a skill that hasn't been required in most markets for several years.

The addition of new product and the proliferation of brands stimulated by increasing demand over the last few years also mean a decline in franchise contribution for many hotels. Ask not what your franchise can do for you – go look in the mirror and figure out what you can do for your hotel in the short term. How can you prepare your property to maintain market share in these circumstances?

1. Evaluate your rate positioning against your competition every day. Adjust your 'drop dead' rates for the night and short lead reservation rates accordingly. Ensure that all reservation sources that can be immediately impacted are notified of any changes that you may make based on your forecast. These include your central reservations system, internet based distribution sources, and central reservations sources for your area such as resort associations. Develop 'fast and dirty' rate driven flyers

for local visitor centers, rest areas and other sources of walk-in and short-lead reservations.

2. Get your sales department out on the road making sales calls. Walking in doors, keeping existing clients close and prospecting for new ones can stimulate short lead demand. Grass roots marketing and sales work in most markets. Encouraging smaller accounts and groups you may not have been interested in last year helps to buttress occupancy. The summer of 2001 is about market share. Evaluate the sales skills of your staff and provide immediate training if they have deficiencies. Ask for and analyze their sales reports. Are they generating leads or only responding to inquiries? Support them in their efforts by accompanying them on sales calls and giving the potential client your personal assurance of quality service for their guests.

3. Empower and motivate the front desk to capture every same day reservation and walk-in. Typically, we suspend incentive programs during the summer because demand is high and we believe that we will capture our share of demand without them. It is far easier for the front desk to let a walk-in go back out the door than to go the extra mile to close them.

4. Give your guests the highest level of service they can imagine – exceed their expectations. Make your expectations of quality customer service clear to your employees in terms of empowering them to satisfy the guest and resolve guest complaints. Don't limit this to the front desk but include all of your employees. Value-add by putting complimentary coffee in the lobby and a bowl of apples on the front desk. Demonstrate to your staff what you mean by modeling customer

service behavior with guests — show the staff your level of commitment to customer service.

In all likelihood, it is going to be a tough summer for a lot of hoteliers. Minimize the damage and maintain or increase your market share against a competitive set that may be 'asleep at the switch' until it is too late. Be proactive and flexible – the race belongs to those that are quick to respond to changing conditions.

Marketing Yourself to Prospective Employees

The competition for employees is intense with so many hospitality establishments trying to recruit from the same labor pool. There is a limit to the hourly wages we can offer. Most establishments offer wages in the same range so money is no longer a compelling issue for these employees. They are a bit spoiled in that this is a generation has never known unemployment. They also know that if this job isn't what they want, they can cross the street and find another job. In this kind of environment it is a matter of 'what's in it for me'.

Motivating and Training a New Generation of Employees, it was noted that the potential employees we are trying to recruit have motivations other than money for working in a certain establishment. They have choices. It's a buyer's market. Hotel sales people are asked to formulate a brief 'value proposition' with which to gain a potential client's interest in the benefits of booking rooms in our hotels. This includes benefit statements tailored to the client's special requirements, not just features, of the hotel.

For those of you who need a refresher on the difference between benefits and features, a feature is an amenity such as the fitness room or pool; the benefit is how that will enhance the experience of the guest. A classic example is the Michelin commercial with the baby in the tire. What is Michelin selling? Not just the feature of the rubber tire but the safety and security that it offers the buyer, the benefit. Micheline is not the least expensive tire on the market and your hotel probably doesn't offer the highest hourly wage. It is important to identify then why an employee would choose to work for you and your hotel. While this may sound easy, it does in fact require some thought.

An effective and honest value proposition can mean potential employees are eager to work for you. If employees are happy working for you, they will tell their friends and soon you will have potential employees calling you for an interview. How easy would that make your recruiting!

As the labor pool becomes tighter, the hospitality industry is dipping deeper into this age group for line employees and lamenting the fact that turnover is high and service levels are low. We often have the specter of employees being driven to work by parents because they don't yet have a driver's license. Managers lament the lack of loyalty and unwillingness for go the extra mile for the 'team'. When confronted with a performance issue, the employee will sometimes just stare at the manager as though he or she is from another planet – in a way, the manager is from another planet if he or she is over thirty.

What's even more frustrating to some hotel managers is Generation Y's total disinterest in 'sucking up' and tendency to bluntly tell the manger and other employees exactly what they think of a situation. They don't even care if you fire them – although they will seldom give a manager the opportunity to terminate them, they just leave!

Implications for the Hospitality Industry

Managers who have succeeded to this point in managing by intimidation and threats won't make it with this generation. This is a generation that has never known unemployment. Work is there for them if they want it. They are in the driver's seat – they choose you. Money isn't the prime motivator – they can get that anywhere. Unlike previous generations that would grumble at being poorly treated but stay for the sake of a paycheck, these workers won't put up with it. Why should they? The onus is on us to make the workplace make sense to them, to keep it interesting and fun.

The smart companies do this. Others have been so overwhelmed by the robust economy, that they have not taken the time to pay attention to these basic principles of good management or they never knew them in first place. In the new economy where managers are struggling to maintain basic levels of customer service with fewer employees, it is difficult to gain a perspective that allows them to plan and execute good recruitment and retention policies, much less a customer service training program that gives them an edge. The consumer is unfortunately beginning to accept mediocre customer service as superior because basic levels of customer service are becoming increasingly rare.

In reading and studying CRM (customer relationship management if you've been in a cave or working the front desk) notice that it is predicated upon accumulating guest history and preferences and solidifying the loyalty of that customer. This is based upon the premise that a retained customer is less expensive than obtaining a new customer. While the above is a marketing truism, what the whole concept assumes is that we are providing the customer service to A) obtain correct information that the customer is experiencing a sufficient level of satisfaction to return. Both of these speak to the issue of customer service training. We assume that if we hire the right people, they will treat the guest well. The paradox of the present is that we may hire the right people but if we don't treat them well, they won't stay long enough to allow us to deliver a consistent level of customer service to the guest.

Culture of Customer Service

As the economy continues to boom and unemployment remains low, customer service is the challenge of the day. We are victims of our own success. The hospitality industry is also struggling with 'increased' loads from more guests and a shortage of employees, as is every other industry that has customers. The retail industry is seeing that people prefer to shop on line in many cases than go to a 'bricks and mortar' store to spend money and be served poorly.Many of them have never made a reservation, never been a guest in a hotel and their F&B experience is limited to fast food. They don't know what we expect in terms of customer service unless we not only make the expectations clear but also treat them as though they are our 'internal' customers and give them the level of service that we expect them to give.

Every organization has a 'culture' of values or 'how things are done'. This includes who gets rewarded in terms of recognition and promotions as well as how we treat each other, both vertically and laterally. This hotel management is one the best at creating a culture of guest service, from ownership through management ranks. One day, however, the auditor passed a card to the Director of Sales saying that this individual had had a problem with housekeeping and could she call the guest. Upon calling upon the guest, it seems that his problems went deeper and included the auditor's response to his complaints.

Most everyone in the industry benefits from summer tourism, with the possible exception of some southern locations and winter resorts. Preliminary numbers indicate that tourism exceeded expectations this summer as the economy continues to boom and travelers may have complained but paid the increased prices for gas and airline tickets. However, a rising tide floats all boats and some of your boats will be beached come the end of September.

What is your current market penetration and yield in relation to your competitive set? When everyone is running full most nights except perhaps Sunday, it is difficult not to look good. Your market share penetration may have increased slightly but this may only be a Band-Aid and not a cure if your market share was ailing prior to the summer season. If your market share has increased by a smaller percentage than that of your competitive set, you may have a problem. If your penetration was below 100% prior to June, what steps have you taken to fix it?

Another important thing to consider, are you giving priority to the customers that will still be there to support you during the off-season, albeit at a lower rate than you might be able to drive from the leisure sector? This leads to the yield management side of the equation where you absolutely need to control your rate and inventory by market segment. Have you designated a set number of rooms to market segments that may be lower rated but will continue to use you the rest of the year?

Studies show that these employees remain at jobs that engage them, where they feel that they have input, that their efforts are appreciated working with people that they like and respect. First of all you have to provide training that gives them the tools to do their jobs. It is a chicken and egg question – should you invest in training them when they are just going to leave in six months or will they leave in six months if you don't train them? Lack of training is rarely cited by the employee in an exit interview, but job satisfaction is increased by knowing how to do the job that you are asked to perform. Think about it. Furthermore, can you estimate how many guests you may have lost or will lose over untrained and unresponsive staff? This is one of the factors driving our customers to alternate distribution channels such as those available on the Internet.

Effective Use of Technology in Hotel Sales

The most common reason cited for this is that it is unnecessary for everyone to be connected because —

— "They will only send email to their friends or surf the net for personal reasons on company time"

— "It allows the GM to screen email they are sending"

— "It is too expensive to upgrade the hardware to make it worthwhile for everyone to be connected".

The proper use of internet based technology not only saves time and makes the salesperson more efficient but the revenue potential of this tool is enormous if only the sales staff and the General Manager truly understand the opportunities it affords and how to manage it to maximize revenue.

Email: Email is the most efficient tool for communication and correspondence yet developed. Most business people use it instead of mail for correspondence and only use 'snail mail' for original documents. It is significant that President Clinton just signed a bill which will make email signatures as legally binding as hard copy originals. FedEx and US Mail look out! However, there is a definite etiquette to email. All emails should be acknowledged within seven to ten days and if the recipient is out of email communication for longer than that, an automatic response should be sent indicating that.

Sentence structure, grammar and spelling are as important in email as they are in traditional correspondence. Spelling and grammar check are not enough and it requires proofing for words and usages that fall through those cracks. Because email is so immediate, it is tempting to become too casual or informal in tone and address. Don't make the mistake of assuming too much familiarity.

Fax: Most computer based contact management systems (you do have an automated contact management program, don't you?) have word processing and an internal fax function. What can demonstrate a sense of urgency and timely follow-up more effectively than faxing a contract or proposal within minutes of hanging up the phone with a client! All documents are neatly stored and transmission records are available to anyone who needs to see them.

Web Site Design and Management: At a time when even six-year-olds have web sites and ten-year-olds can design and build them, what differentiates yours from the masses? How does yours get noticed in the plethora of sites that appear when the key words 'hotel', your franchise and your location are entered? Does your site look like a brochure that was scanned in or has it been given sufficient thought so that the design conveys the impression of your property that will appeal to your customer demographic?

How are the pages arranged – do you give enough information to differentiate you from the competition or do you simply repeat the obvious? Upon what server does your site reside? Have you built in enough hyperlinks, to which sites and what response mechanisms have you built in? Who monitors responses? Does your host server ensure that your site is refreshed monthly with the major search engines so that it continues to appear within the top fifty to one hundred responses for the key words you have selected?

Maximizing the Internet connection for sales

1. *Research.* It used to be that in order to research a corporate account, one had to request the annual report or ask twenty questions to the primary contact and hope that they were forthcoming with accurate information. Most associations can be accessed by .org and companies by .com. If ten-year-olds have web sites, you can be assured that many if not most SMERF groups even have them. If they have adopted a difficult acronym ask what their site is called or it usually appears on the business card. Now one can access the web site and discover who the major players are, the corporate or organizational values (read between the lines) and what they actually do or make. This is invaluable information for making an effective sales

call. It may even contain information on when and where their last meetings were held. Their web site may also contain information about trade associations, industry publications and their last newsletter may be archived.

2. *Prospecting.* It is a huge concern that in some markets, the sales people are so overwhelmed with responding to inquiries, they tell me that they don't have the time to prospect. The net effect of this is that the client chooses the hotel not the hotel choosing the client based on its prerequisites. The web allows sales people to search for prospects based on the hotel's 'ideal client' profile (please tell me that you have given some thought to what your 'ideal client' looks like). You can access data and slice it through key word searches to identify prospects that you can further research. You can even communicate with these prospects via email and express interest in hosting their next meeting or becoming their hotel of choice – how is that for creative prospecting!

3. *Meeting Marketplaces.* Many hospitality web platforms now have a meeting marketplace service where companies and organizations enter their requirements and for a fee, hotels can access the database, decide which ones they can best serve and bid on the business. Newmarket International's MeetingBroker.com is one of these.

4. *RFP Processing.* There are programs and even web sites that specialize in sorting and tracking a hotel's response to an RFP. You can access potential bids, decide whether or not to bid, track the date of the submission and responses.

5. *Travel Related Web Sites.* More and more leisure and corporate travelers are using the web to locate hotels in selected destinations. These include discount sites such as Priceline and Travelocity and there are a host of others, some that cater to a specific demographic. If you haven't sorted through these by price and client base, you are missing the boat and the boat is growing larger every day. However, all of these sites require management and timely response mechanisms from your property. It is imperative that you have designated a person or department to monitor inventory, rate and responsiveness in order to maximize your revenue from these sites. You also need to be selective and make decisions based on price and the site's ability to deliver to your property based on your requirements.

There are three distinct areas that can assist management in measuring sales effectiveness;

— Defining the areas to be evaluated;

— Monitoring sales performance in relation to the above areas and

— Designing incentives to reflect Management's goals for the property.

The current employment climate in the hotel industry has put severe limitations on the ability of hotels to recruit and retain sales people with sales experience and/or a background in hotels. In many cases, we are promoting from within, usually the front desk, or relying on intuition that untried recruits are trainable. This situation is even more apparent in the limited to moderate service sectors, that is, non-convention hotels reliant on their local markets to generate the majority of their demand.

Compounding the situation in the limited and moderate service sectors are decreasing occupancies in both the limited service and all suite sectors for 1999. This makes an effective sales effort more critical at a time when flat revenues limit the resources a property or management company has to retain qualified sales and marketing professionals.

In the current climate, we are dealing with sales people often with no experience, whose longevity with the property is relatively brief, often only nine to eighteen months. With little training and a steep learning curve, it becomes the 'deep end of the pool' training. That is, we throw them into the deep end of the pool and wait on the side. If they float, we figure they will make it. The other side of the coin is that with such a short average duration on the job, many companies are reluctant to spend the dollars sending them to training.

With a high degree of turnover and a shortage of recruits, sales positions, both at the property and corporate levels are left open for long periods of time. Any sales momentum is lost and clients have difficulty being serviced. In addition, many 'experienced' sales people were never taught the basic steps of the sales process or how to completely penetrate their markets. Those whose experience has been in the years between 1992-98, the 'boom' years, were primarily managing the yield from increased demand prior to the entry of new hotel product into their respective markets and may have little experience in generating demand from market penetration and additional revenue from existing accounts.

Understanding what new sales people are looking for from an employment situation is crucial to maximizing both longevity and training. Studies show that they are not there for the money alone, and we all know that the salaries in the hotel sales field have not kept pace with the rest of the marketplace. On the one hand, they want to feel part of a team, that their input and opinions are solicited and valued but on the other, they want to know what's in it for them, in terms of rewards for performance and career potential. When an inexperienced recruit is left untrained, they become frustrated and are easy prey for the competition or other industries.

As well, clients have become fickle and, with overbuilding in this sector, will switch to a new hotel for a few dollars less in rate or a newer hotel product with additional amenities such as a two room suite for the price of a room at a traditional property. They have also become cynical about building relationships with sales people due to the turnover factor. The days are also gone when most companies can drive all of their business to one hotel. Their employees are demanding more flexibility based on their preferences and frequent guest programs, when location and rate are relatively similar. The traditional 'booker' now exerts influence but can not always guarantee the choices that an employee will make.

It is now more important than ever to 'spread the risk' of losing revenue from several key accounts to a total market penetration strategy that includes smaller companies which, if the company's fortunes change, will not take the hotel's revenue base down with it. One need look no further than the Seattle area when Boeing was downsizing and restructuring to see an example of an entire market's dependency on one key account. Those hotels that had built a broad customer base fared better than those that didn't.

An examination of a hotel's source of business report usually reveals that while a few accounts can be identified that produce a large number of rooms, it is usually no more than 15 to 20% of a hotel's occupied rooms, the majority of the rest being frequent guest programs or unidentified 'corporate' and 'discount'. The old 80/20 rule does not necessarily apply anymore. In a corporate market, up to 80% of your business now comes from 'independents', employees of larger companies that when location is equal will stay where their frequent guest points are and contractors and consultants who will make their own decisions based on the same factors. The 'independent' client is difficult to identify and woo but not impossible.

Reducing the learning curve and enabling sales people to generate revenue for the hotel in the shortest period of time is the goal of effective training and should be conducted as soon as possible following the recruitment of a new sales person. Whether training occurs in a seminar setting or one-on-one, results should be tangible in terms of a sales person's immediate effectiveness and quantifiable in terms of additional revenue generation within 60 days after it is completed. It should include on-going reinforcement through the Internet or, if unavailable, more traditional methods such as conference calls and availability to counsel via e-mail or telephone. A newsletter with concrete sales 'tools' that sales people can implement keeps the basic concepts fresh in their minds.

Those hotels and management companies that take training seriously can reduce turnover and retain staff longer than the average. Recruitment and retention will continue to be a problem for the foreseeable future, which is why training needs to be ongoing and constantly reinforced. The General Managers need to be included in the process as often they are the only ones on property to sell and have the responsibility of overseeing the sales effort every day. Incentives for sales and GMs based on property revenue keeps everyone focused on the goal.

Every hotel and motel manager makes mistakes; that's just part of being human. All mistakes are costly; but some have a greater financial impact than others do. The following list cites potentially costly security gaps most hoteliers are not aware of or haven't focused on - and should.

1. *Never cut back on security personnel.* In these times of cost containment and budget controls, security is the one area of your budget that should never be cut. The financial impact of reducing or eliminating your security staff would be tremendous should a guest or employee be injured or damage to property occur. In addition, eliminating or reducing security personnel sends the wrong message to staff members, namely that their safety is not of the highest importance to your business and that you are not watching them as closely.

2. *Have an evacuation route posted in your meeting room space.* Meeting rooms serve as gathering places for large groups of people who will most likely panic in the event of an emergency such as a hurricane, earthquake, bomb threat and so on. In the event of a crisis, will your group function attendees know where to go and what to do? Have evacuation routes posted in meeting rooms for group attendees to see, and ask your sales and catering personnel to have detailed discussions with the meeting planners about evacuation procedures.

3. *Increase lighting throughout your property.* Look for physical areas on or around the property that do not have adequate lighting or are not secure, and address these issues immediately. Check your parking lots for areas where lighting needs improvement. Ask your local law enforcement agency to do a security audit on your property. Don't wait until someone falls or is injured to protect your guests, employees and your business.

4. *Continuously train employees.* When it rains or snows and a guest slips and falls on your property, do your employees know the proper steps to take to protect the injured guest, not to make casual comments admitting liability and how to handle the situation? Who is responsible for their training? Make it your objective to ensure that your employees receive adequate training on procedures for handling guest injuries. Initial training and continuous ongoing training are critical. One hour of training is not enough. Keep detailed records of the procedures and training which can be used in your efforts to convince a litigious opposing party, and a judge, of your due diligence in safety training.

5. *Comply with Occupational Safety and Health Administration standards.* Make sure all OSHA requirements and standards are met. If you are not sure that you have all the latest information, take an updated course on compliance efforts. The Internet has many resources for OSHA compliance courses available for hotels and motels. Visually inspect to see that all necessary notices and posters are current and displayed appropriately, and not stuck behind other notices on the bulletin board.

6. *Keep back-up data off property.* Keep a copy of all property operations data stored off-site in a safe and secure location. Do not rely on someone's personal computer to house your employment, financial and guest data. It is imperative to have access to guest records at all times - especially in the event of an emergency.
7. *Install phones in fitness centers.* All exercise or fitness rooms need to have a phone available to all guests that will dial immediately to the front desk. A security camera should also be installed so that injuries and problems that occur within the fitness facility can be immediately detected and addressed. If security cameras are used, written procedures for their use must be in place. Also: Are the cameras staffed with trained professionals viewing the scene? How often is the videotape reused? Are the cameras in good working order or are they simply mounted as a decoy to provide a false sense of security to guests and employees?
8. *Perform background checks on employees before hiring.* All managers, front desk personnel and security officers must have their background history checked to eliminate or minimize any unknown and undesirable discoveries once employed. An Internet search can assist in accomplishing this task very quickly. Check driving records on employees hired to transfer guests to and from the airport or surrounding areas. Select the best employees now and avoid future trouble.
9. *Check detection devices regularly.* Are sprinkler systems and smoke detectors working and in place, on all floors, in guestrooms and in all public spaces? Is an emergency lighting system in place along with an

emergency generator? When was the last time you had these items checked? What is your back up plan if these devices should fail? All such items need to be tested and certified on a monthly basis and the inspections need to be properly documented in writing.

10. *Check on emergency equipment periodically.* Does your property have automatic external defibrillators and oxygen tanks on site and are they in working order? Have employees been trained to use these devices? Make sure you conduct monthly inspections on these types of equipment, and have at least one CPR-trained employee on staff at all times.

These are but a few of the safety precautions being overlooked by many hotel and motels around the country. Preventative measures are always preferred over litigation strategies. Your guests and employees expect and want an injury-free experience and work environment. Implementing these steps, and reviewing them on a continuous basis, will go a long way in protecting your business.

Preventing Legal Attacks

How can you dramatically reduce legal attacks while building a wall of defense around your company? Follow these ten simple steps and you will be on your way to protecting your company by building a fortress of defense.

1. *Investigate and take action on all reports of harassment and discrimination.* All managers and directors must report to the human resources director or other personnel any and all incidences or claims made by employees in

connection with sexual harassment or any other type of harassment or discrimination. If managers do not report the incident or claim and an investigation does not occur, the company is at risk. Every employee should undergo annual anti-harassment and anti-discrimination training. The company's policy of prohibiting harassment and discrimination of any kind should be clear, in writing, and effectively communicated to every employee. Newly hired employees, as well as seasoned veterans, need this training. During any investigation, if new incidences are discovered, those incidences should also be thoroughly investigated. A report, which includes written statements of witnesses and the resolution of the claims, needs to be well documented and placed in the appropriate personnel file.

2. *Make sure all agreements with vendors and suppliers are in writing and their insurance has not expired.* The financial officer of each hotel or restaurant should undertake a careful review of all agreements. Be particularly mindful of indemnification clauses (in which one person agrees to protect another person from claims by third parties), waivers and releases, automatic renewals of the term of the agreement and assignment clauses that prohibit the hotel or restaurant from transferring the agreement to a new purchaser or new operator. Make sure all vendor and supplier agreements allow for the hotel or restaurant to cancel for any reason or no reason on thirty-(30) day's written notice. Obtain current certificates of insurance from every vendor and supplier and ask for updated certificates periodically. Make certain that the insurance certificate lists the hotel or restaurant

operating or managing company, as well as the owner of the establishment, as additional insured parties on the policy.

3. *Keep accurate maintenance logs on all equipment.* Many cases have been settled or lost in court due to the failure of the property owner to maintain accurate maintenance logs on equipment owned or serviced by a hotel. This includes the monthly, quarterly or annual maintenance checks on elevators, bicycles, fitness equipment, pool equipment, etc. It is important to maintain clear and accurate records to show a judge, jury or opposing lawyer the diligence that went in to ensuring the property was safe. Among other things, the records should reflect the times and dates of inspection, any and all repairs made and the name(s) of the qualified employee(s) responsible for maintaining the records. Accidents happen, of course, but an accurate maintenance log will go a long way in reducing your liability.

4. *Follow all rules for proper notification to guests of in-room telephone charges.* Due to the popularity of cell phones and PDAs, hotel guestroom telephone usage has declined. However, many hoteliers may not be aware that there are federal and state laws stating what must be clearly communicated to your guests prior to them making telephone calls from guestrooms. Written notice of all fees and charges must be given to the callers in the guestrooms as directed by the statutes, and should be featured in a prominent location. The in-room guest directory should include the following information and applicable charges: local calls, directory assistance, alternate carrier access (for other long distance carriers than the one the hotel does

business with), toll free calls, international calls and long distance calls.

5. *Don't send unsolicited faxes to customers without their written permission.* The 1991 Federal Telephone Consumer Protection Act prohibits the sending of unsolicited fax advertisements in all states. Specifically, business owners are not allowed to send unsolicited faxes that advertise the commercial availability or quality of property, goods or services to customers without first obtaining their permission. The recipient of such faxes can successfully sue the sender and collect $500 per fax. Plus, if they can prove you willfully violated the law, they could recover $1500 per violation. Although some companies are challenging this law based on First Amendment issues, until the law is changed, compliance will eliminate these claims.

6. *Have all employees who pour, serve or sell alcohol beverages, and all managers, attend an alcohol awareness program.* Not only is it important for this training to occur, your legal adviser (and most likely, your insurance carrier) will insist that your employees learn the legal basics of pouring, serving and selling alcohol beverages to your patrons and guests. Most states have "dram shop laws" that require establishments to adhere to alcohol safety and awareness standards. If someone leaves your establishment and is personally injured or injures another person or property, the patron's lawyer will look to the establishment to see if alcohol was consumed on the premises. Be smart and implement preventative measures now.

7. *Have a written email policy prohibiting jokes, off-color remarks, and other potentially offensive activities.* As part of their lawsuits against companies, plaintiffs are

requesting that defendant companies produce all email transmissions in order to collection incriminating information about the company and its employees. These messages, although may appear to be deleted by each user, are not gone forever. They actually are maintained on back-up tapes that carry this information forever (at least a very long time until they are erased by an IT professional). Remind employees that although email messages appear to be a quick and casual way of communicating, it can be hazardous to your company's bottom line. Advise them not to put anything in an email message that they would not want to see as a headline in your daily newspaper. Every company's written email policy should require all employees to avoid creating, viewing or forwarding offensive or inappropriate emails or Internet postings related to a person's race, color, national origin, religion, sex, sexual orientation, age, disability or veteran status. Also, they should avoid creating, viewing or forwarding jokes, cartoon, games or chain letters. The email policy should also provide for immediate disciplinary action or termination of employment, if necessary, for violations.

8. *Be aware of scams.* There are numerous scams ongoing for many years that managers need to be aware of and need to educate all employees. For example, con artists are targeting companies with the Nigerian letter scam. This scam begins with a letter or message that is mailed, faxed or emailed informing a business that there is a certain surplus of funds that exist and by providing your business bank account information to hold these funds for a short time, the business will receive a portion of these funds. This is an attempt to

empty your company's bank account. Also, be aware that certain companies may be marketing a hotel directory that is not pre-approved or in line with your company's marketing strategies. An unsuspecting employee may obligate your company by agreeing to a long-term commitment to have your property listed in the directory.

9. *Inform your guests about laptop computer theft*. In too many cases, laptop computers are left in hotel meeting rooms and are easy targets for thieves. To anticipate your guest's needs, provide a safe to store laptop computers when not in use or when the group is taking a break from their meeting. Provide computer-cabling locks to assist your guests in securing their laptops. Lock or control entry to meeting rooms when not in use. While not a preventative measure, hoteliers can also post a warning in the area so that the hotel is not responsible for stolen or damaged property. Prior to posting the sign, review your state's limitation of liability statute to determine your liability in such cases.

10. *Don't release guest information to anyone other than the guest*. Releasing guest information to the wrong person can result in a claim being filed against your property. Guests have a certain expectation of privacy that needs to be acknowledged and recognized by all employees. A written policy needs to be established whereby (i) the registered guest makes the request in person and either the guest is recognized by the employee or provides sufficient identification or (ii) the guest submits a signed, written request and the hotel or motel is able to verify that the signature belongs to the registered guest. Certain exceptions to the policy

would include those circumstances when the hotel or motel is compelled by law to produce the guest information (a court order or subpoena, for example) or when a crime has been committed against the hotel or motel.

Safe from Theifs

Identity theft can occur in hotels and motels and should be taken very seriously. In US, the Federal Trade Commission has stated that identity fraud is one of the fastest growing white-collar crimes nationwide and affects one in four Americans. In 2002, the FTC received 161,819 complaints about identity theft and it is estimated that it costs each victim more than $1,000 to correct the damage made to their accounts and their reputations. Identity thieves capture information about your guests and use it to commit fraud, steal money, and charge items to credit accounts and even create new accounts. How can you protect your patrons and guests from being victims of identity theft? Here are some basic security rules for you to pass on to your managers and supervisors to decrease the likelihood that your patrons and guests will be the next victims of identity theft.

— Training is the most important rule. Hotel personnel should never announce out loud the guest's name and room number at the front desk during check-in or in the food and beverage outlets in the hotel or facility. If during the check-in process, you or any of your employees overhears a guestroom number being announced, immediately assign a different room for the guest. In addition, instruct your wait staff not to request a guest's room number out loud in restaurants. Have the guest write it on a piece of paper then destroy the paper. Never, ever say the room number out loud. Believe it or not, this is still happening at hotels and motels across America.

— Instruct your housekeeping staff to leave a kind note for the guest reminding them to never leave important papers containing personal information in plain view in your guestroom, the lobby, any of the food and beverage outlets or in any meeting room space. Remind them to put all personal information, such as airplane tickets, passports, etc. in the in-room safe located in the guestroom when absent from the room.

— Remind guests, and meeting planners so they can advise their attendees, to make sure all computers, including laptops and PDAs (which usually contain valuable and personal information) are secured in all meeting rooms or hand carried by the owner from the guestroom or meeting room space.

— Have your front office and accounting office procedures that address your efforts to safeguard guests' personal information in writing and available for your guests to see. Find out if there are any leaks or holes in your process. Who has access to guests' data and is it secured? Are the employees trained on maintaining the privacy of guests, and how so and how often? How secure are your fax machines? Does personal guest information lie around for anyone walking by to see? Hotels and motels need to focus on these issues and if you haven't, you need to do so immediately.

— Do not place calls directly to guestrooms without the caller knowing the name of the guest assigned to the guestroom for that day. Although your telephone operators want to be helpful to callers, they should never give out names or partial names of any guests to outside callers.

— Do not slip guestroom folios under the guestroom doors the evening prior to checkout. Mistakes by your night shift hotel staff can and do happen and valuable personal information may find it's way into another guestroom or worse yet, stranded in the middle of the hallway for all guests and employees to see.

— Check the credit card receipts printed from all outlets in your hotel, such as retail shops and restaurants. Some receipts still print the entire credit card numbers. Others only print the last four digits of the credit card number. Having the entire number printed on the receipt can be hazardous to your guests' financial health. This is usually a simple software programming issue and it will protect your guests if you promptly remedy this situation.

— Remind all meeting attendees to remove their convention badges outside the meeting venue as it provides immediate personal information to any stranger the attendee passes by. Also, remind meeting planners to be careful as to what information is stored on the back side of the convention badges because if it is lost or misplaced, the information displayed, albeit intended for the ease and convenience of the attendee (such as cell phone numbers of colleagues), can end up in the wrong hands.

— Inspect your wastepaper refuse system or trash dumpsters for your hotel or facility. It is in a secure area? Is it inaccessible to the general public? Does a fence or wall surround it? If thieves will go through your personal household trash receptacles to gain personal information, imagine what they could find if they gained access to the waste paper dumpster located at your hotel or motel. Some thieves have admitted that they go dumpster diving at accounting and law offices to gain proprietary information. What will they find if they dive into your dumpsters?

— Be aware of the potential for identity theft with your hotel if you engage shoptalk or shop call systems. This is when you contract with a third party provider to record live reservation calls for purposes of spot checking the reservation agents for compliance efforts and for training purposes. These audio recordings which include names, addresses and credit card information are now in the hands of someone, other than the hotel staff, that can abuse the process and use this information to steal personal information. Make sure you have written agreements with these companies, together with clear and precise language in the contracts prohibiting any type of use of the information contained on the tapes. The information on the tapes should be limited to hotel use only.

Bibliography

Arnold, R., Davies, S, and Pearce, D., "Some Economic Implications of Tourism Expansion: Inquiry into Travel and Tourism, *Discussion Paper No. 2*, Australian Government Publishing Service, Canberra, 1989.

Arzeni, S., "International tourism: Past trends and prospects", *IIEC Discussion Paper,* 1989.

Bockstael, N.E., Strand, I.E. and Hanemann, W.M., "Time and Recreational Demand Model", *American Journal of Agricultural Economics,* Vol. 69 (2), pp. 293-302, 1987.

Barkin, David, "Distorted Development: Mexico in the World Economy", *Westview,* Boulder, CO., 1990.

Browne, R.J., and Nolan, M.L., "Western Indian Reservation Tourism Development", *Annals of Tourism Research, Vol. 16* (3), pp. 360-376, 1989.

Burkart, A.J. and Medlik, S., *Tourism: past, present and future,* Heinemann, London, 1974.

Butler, R.W., "The concept of a tourist area cycle of evolution: Implications for the management of resources", *Canadian Geographer,* Vol. 24., pp. 5-12, 1980.

Kasper, C., "Recent developments in tourism research and education at the university level", in S. Witt and L. Moutinho, *Tourism Marketing and Management Handbook,* New York, Prentice Hall, 1989.

Koh, K., "Designing the four-year tourism management curriculum: a marketing approach", *Journal of Travel Research*, Summer, pp. 68-72, 1995.

Lundberg, C., "A prolegomen to course design in hospitality management: Fundamental considerations", *Journal of Hospitality and Tourism Education*, 10(2): 26-30

Messenger, S., "The UK hospitality and tourism industry; an overview of the issues affecting the supply of education and training in the 1990s", in C. Cooper (ed.), Progress in Tourism Recreation and Hospitality Management Vol. III, London, Belhaven, 1991.

Parsons, D., "The making of managers", *Lessons from an international review of tourism management education programmes*, Tourism Management, 12(3), 1991

Index